# THE MILLENNIAL MOM

## Balancing the Messy Life of A Modern Woman

# THE MILLENNIAL MOM

## Balancing the Messy Life of A Modern Woman

## SHIKHA KEDIA BHARADWAJ

Worldwide Publishing by

**Pendown** Press

Powered by Gullybaba

**PENDOWN PRESS**
*Powered by* **Gullybaba Publishing House Pvt. Ltd.,**
**An ISO 9001 & ISO 14001 Certified Co.,**
**Regd. Office:** 2525/193, 1st Floor, Onkar Nagar-A, Tri Nagar,
Delhi-110035
**Ph.:** 09350849407, 09312235086
**E-mail:** info@pendownpress.com
**Branch Office:** 1A/2A, 20, Hari Sadan, Ansari Road,
Daryaganj, New Delhi–110002
**Ph.:** 011-45794768
**Website:** PendownPress.com

**First Edition:** 2022

**ISBN:** 978-93-5554-012-6



*Cover, Layout and Illustrations by* Pendown Graphics Team
*Printed and Bound in India by* Thomson Press India Ltd.

# Dedication

*I dedicate this book to my Grandmother. I know she is smiling and watching me from wherever she is. She will always be a part of my heartbeat :).*

# Contents

# Foreword

The most important part of being a woman and a mother is that, at any given point, we need to raise our children with the belief that they are enough. This awareness only comes through accepting that truth ourselves. As mothers, our core responsibility is to nurture the new lives that we helped create and raise them to become complete entities of their own. Shikha's narrative helps us practically embrace this fact.

While we might embrace our roles as mothers, we need to realise that we are also women, daughters-in-law, wives, career women, and so much more. These roles define us, and we try hard to be our best, to excel in them every single day, but at times we tend to procrastinate in some areas, and others can get neglected. Shikha blends this constant inner battle that women face in a matter of fact and humour to bring out the nuances of urban living.

We need to remember that we are enough and should be guilt-free when working on ourselves, our careers, and our families. You can be guilt-free only if, just like your breath, you let go of everything you are holding on to. If you are holding on to your breath and constantly telling yourself that you are good enough to achieve this or able to do that, you will not be able to let go of the guilt you feel.

All women want is to be guilt-free parents and have guilt-free careers. This is why they need to take stock of their actions and plan things through goal setting, whether conceptually or creatively. If there are certain activities you can't perform, let them go, and make the best out of the 24 hours you and everyone else have. There will always be someone who accomplishes more than you, and there will always be someone who accomplishes less than you.

Similarly, there will always be someone you think is a better mother than you and someone you feel isn't. The author here points to the fact that motherhood isn't something you can compare because there will always be a better or worse; it only depends on how much you do with your unique set of skills and what you can bring to the table in your life.

This is why we need to do mindfulness practices every day. Mindfulness practices can be as simple as waking up and breathing for five minutes, using sound and chanting, writing affirmations, and visualising meditation to see where we are and where we want to be and be in touch with ourselves for greater self-awareness.

Self-awareness leads to balance within the self and for people living in your vicinity and environment. It helps us let go of things holding us back that stop us from enjoying ourselves. A balanced life does not mean constantly running around to complete tasks for work, children, or the home. I try to find this self-awareness by scheduling 'stop and enjoy' time daily. I take this time for myself and spend it either listening to music, dancing, or reading. Sometimes, I take a cup of tea and just stare out of the window. It might feel clinical to schedule it, but if you don't, you will procrastinate on the time you want to stop and enjoy because the mind doesn't advocate for time spent just on yourself and your thoughts.

I have been a Bharatnatyam dancer, and classical dance has taught me that we need to be resilient, diligent, and disciplined to find our core and centre and keep building on that, learning bit by bit by taking small steps every day. Maintaining the centre is very important, and the centre is within yourself. If you can maintain your peace, calm, patience, and be resilient, everything around you will keep falling back into balance, even if it goes off track and becomes turbulent from time to time.

You have to know your core competencies as an individual, which have nothing to do with being a mother or a working person, a housewife or a homemaker. Instead, it has to do with who you are, how you have been raised, how you have trained yourself through your education, work, hobbies, etc. Once you know who you are, what your competencies are- whether it be your kinaesthetic or listening skills, your ability to plan or create, you need to accept your strengths and limitations and seek help from others to allow your child to reach their true potential. You need to recognise the need to delegate childcare as it does take a village to raise a child. If you ask people for help, you will find that you have more time to plan, making motherhood a not so frustrating experience. You don't have to learn everything all at one time when you become a parent.

Every day, we face certain situations that are achievements and others which feel like failures. When you begin to focus on your losses, you start to harbour resentment and negativity. So, I would recommend that at the end of every day, always count your accomplishments and write down what you're grateful for because it will help you recognise what you have achieved and are thankful for at all times. This way, any baggage you may have will not get carried forward to the next day.

Also, forgiveness is divine. So, forgive whoever seems to have troubled you – be it your child, your house help, a worker, someone in a taxi, a stranger on the road, anybody. Forgive yourself for not being able to respond to them in the proper manner or for not being equal to the task at that time, and forgive the other person who may have caused you any minor or major distress. You can also try unloading your day on a piece of paper or in the fire. The activity of penning down all the negative thoughts or feelings pent up inside you on a piece of paper, torn and burned away, will help you get rid of any baggage that you carry.

We need to start our days being mindful and should end them by being grateful, unloading negative thoughts, and counting our blessings and achievements. That is how you feel centred and balanced every day as a woman creating a new life for herself, her children, family, and the people she influences in her workspace and beyond that in the global community.

This book is an ode to all the roles women play, without the preaching and lecturing. A light-hearted experiential narrative of the reality of working urban mothers, it makes one ponder:

As we juggle all our roles, do we turn into supermoms or circus clowns?

**– Vidhi Beri**
*(Alternative & Holistic Health Service)*

# Acknowledgement

As Sudha Murthy once said, behind every successful woman is an understanding man. This is why I want to start by thanking my husband, Rahul, for always encouraging me to challenge myself and forever being the wind beneath my wings.

Aryan, my son, is my lucky charm. People say that life after a child takes a slow ride in terms of your career and travel plans, but with me, it's been the exact opposite. In the 6 years of having had him in my life, I am the most successful I have ever been in my career. I have travelled to over 20 countries with my little one (this number could have increased, but thanks to Mr. COVID, we could not even step out of our abode, let alone leave the country). Thank you for being so mature and bringing so much happiness into my life.

Nothing in my life would be complete without thanking my mom Uma Kedia for investing so much trust in me. She calls me her "SHERNI" (tigress), and my ability to balance life is a gift she has passed down to me.

My mother-in-law, Shalini Bharadwaj, once said that people always thank their mothers for their achievements, but I want to take this opportunity to tell her that in you, I have always seen a mother. Thank you for being who you are.

I'd also like to give a big virtual hug to my Maa (Grandmother) for loving us all so much. Even while typing this, I shed a tear, remembering the lovely memories I have of her.

A special shout-out to a dear friend and confidante, Vidhi Beri; thank you for helping me at every step and encouraging me to write this book.

This book would have remained a dream without my beautiful editors, Vidushi Duggal and Mehtab Kahlon. I would not have done this without you two.

Finally, to my family, friends and colleagues who have actively or passively contributed to the process of writing this book, you know who you are. Thank you for everything.

# 1

# Moms Vs Societal Double Standards

*"Just because you're not society's idea of perfect doesn't mean you're not!"*

**– Shikha Kedia Bharadwaj –**

Let me start off by reminding all of you reading the book that this is a judgement-free space. I'm here to help you balance your lives better, not to provide you with the secret to round chapatis and happy husbands.

Contrary to what the Internet and well-meaning family and friends might tell you, there is no right way to be a mother. There is, however, an urgent need for discussion when we talk about the pressure and guilt mainstream society puts on parents, especially mothers, to be perfect.

## The Perils of Traditional Societal Roles

There is a clear difference in attitude towards how we Indians traditionally treat roles of both women and men in the household: the man being the provider and the mother, the homemaker. While it is very easy to criticise how outdated this ideology is (especially in the 21$^{st}$ century), it's also impossible to argue that there are certain responsibilities in a household that, to this day, remain gender-specific.

I don't know if you've noticed, but women are not likely to be the sole income providers for their families. As much as one would believe otherwise, having a career for a married woman is always a choice. They get to choose whether they want to do something or not and whether they should monetise on those opportunities.

Men, unfortunately, don't have the freedom of making that same choice. It is an unspoken expectation that they remain responsible for providing financial security for their families. If they choose otherwise, they are made to feel emasculated for their decisions. At this point, I have already angered some of my readers without meaning to. So let me clear up my stance a bit. Fitting into societal expectations is not my cup of tea — the thought of normalising households where both partners work and take on domestic chores definitely is.

An example of such a prevalent double standard is how society at large treats working mothers. A woman can be doing her best to keep everyone at work and home happy and yet be shamed if she cannot take on certain household responsibilities due to her precarious balancing act. In that case, she is considered a failure in the eyes of the family's elders for not being domestic enough.

I remember when my son was about thirteen months old, I had to go on a work trip, which was incidentally also the first time I was going to be away from him. My mother was very apprehensive about me leaving him. She told me that raising my son should be my main priority, not my career. The guilt I felt in parting from my baby for the first time after birth was already at its peak, and my mother (obviously unknowingly) ignited the spark even more. While my mother has since come to realise that women can do it all, it was not an easy mindset to shift.

The truth is that disparity in traditional societal gender roles can be detrimental to a person's wellbeing. However, when it comes to dealing with people who suffer from stagnant ideologies, I have found that letting your actions speak for you is the best way to prove your point. When you dare to pave a path not many others have, people talk. My advice: don't react in the heat of the moment and take what they say with a pinch of salt. It's only a matter of time before those backhanded compliments become admiring well-wishes.

## The Guilty Mother

Motherhood can be emotionally exhausting, especially when you are a first-time mother. When I had given birth five years back, I was a vulnerable wreck that was very harsh on herself. As a new mom, one is extremely sensitive to every comment and thought that comes their way. That vulnerability is a result of society's need to put mothers on pedestals. It is easy to feel lost and diminished as a mother when you cannot reach the impossible motherhood ideals and standards set forth by our own mothers.

Guilt, especially internal guilt, is an emotion every mother is all too familiar with. For working mothers, this guilt can be tenfold. I remember a time when a client, now a treasured friend, had come over to my office for a meeting. My son had been napping on a sofa in my office the whole time; when I suggested moving to a conference room to discuss work further.

While she said nothing then, she recently told me that she had initially judged me heavily for leaving my son alone in my office at the time. I was shocked. My friend had judged me because she thought I was 'quite a carefree mother'. However, she also said that she has since come to genuinely appreciate how I handled the situation then.

Receiving backlash from other mothers is very common. The norm for most mothers is to make their child their biggest priority at all times. When you don't fit the standard, you become susceptible to judgement from others around you.

My advice to guilt-ridden working mothers: Stop already! Nobody forced you to have a career; you made that decision all on your own! It is perfectly natural and instinctual to want to care for your family but stop going on a self-induced guilt trip because of it. Your priorities depend entirely on you. Instead of letting negative feelings take over, prove to yourself and others that your choices do not limit your capability as a mother.

## Making Peace with Yourself

The term "bad mother" is an oxymoron. Every mother raises her children her own way, and as long as what she's doing is in her child's best interests, then God forbid negativity from well-meaning aunties and anyone else. The reality that most of us don't like to accept is that people can only make you feel guilty about things if you feel guilty from within. Your thoughts are feelings you are projecting from within.

As a mother, you are always unsure of the choices you are making. The guilt starts when you start second-guessing your decisions, especially when they are at odds with traditional child-rearing methods. It is easy to judge yourself for things that haven't even happened yet. Your baby's developmental milestones are not a competition to figure out what kind of adults they'll turn out to be in the future. Your children will blossom under your tutelage regardless of these insecurities. Trusting your instincts is a crucial aspect of motherhood.

Personally, for me, raising a child exposed to multiple cultures has been such an interesting journey and a joy to witness. In fact, my approach to unconventional motherhood has ended up working to my son's advantage. While raising him away from family is not easy, it has been well worth the effort to see him grow into the kid he is now. He's independent, and people around me are now patting me on the back for how well I'm raising my son. All the guilt and judgement I faced earlier disappears when I see my son mapping out his path in life. It makes being a mother worth it.

# 2

# Moms Vs The Weight of Expectations

*"A society's expectations of women are a reflection of its belief in their capabilities and value."*

**– H.M. Queen Rania –**

As a teenager in the 2000s, I grew up on Bollywood movies like *Kabhi Khushi, Kabhi Gham, Kuch Kuch Hota Hai*, etc. Jaya Bacchan was Bollywood's version of the ideal Indian mother, and I often wondered why my own mother never welcomed me back from school with an aarti every day. That was then. Now, as I answer a work phone call with Aryan swinging on my back while simultaneously making a cup of coffee, I wonder: Why are we all okay with the media glorifying an unrealistic narrative of motherhood?

Society today lacks a realistic representation of mothers in mainstream media, leading many women to have a skewed view of what mothers are expected to be in real life. Motherhood is a part of a woman's life, not her entire identity. It's not an easy truth to accept, especially since after giving birth, motherhood seems to become the primary role of her life. As I've mentioned before, my mother was very hesitant about me going back to work after my son was born. Not because she was wrong in her way of thinking, but rather because she believed it was the proper way of life.

Women today have done and experienced so much more in life and cannot live the lives our mothers and grandmothers did. While they devoted their whole lives to us as mothers and to their husbands as wives, we cannot be expected to be the same way in today's day and age. I am not demonising society for being stuck in its tracks. There isn't any right or wrong in such matters. The mismatch in expectations of both mothers and their external surroundings can only be cleared if the mother is willing to hear the other party out and make informed decisions without bias.

The reality is that when it comes to dealing with unrealistic expectations, mothers need to start by looking inwards and introspecting. Self-expectations are essentially the manifestation of guilt mothers build up from within. The constant pressure of feeling like you need to be the best mom ever is exceptionally high. This is especially true for mothers who have just given birth. These mothers take on too many expectations all at once and end up experiencing burnout and guilt. Even a small thing like not producing enough milk may feel like an indication that you don't love your child enough.

Negative emotions like these are made so much more powerful after birth and can trigger negative thoughts and expectations that burden mothers even further. It's not a big deal if your child skips a meal or eats poorly for one day. It is fine if your child fell over or got hurt. More than that, it's okay not to feel like you're handling things perfectly all the time. As cliche as it sounds, the single most important thing a woman can do to battle these expectations is prioritising and loving herself.

## Overcompensating at Home

This section is for the mothers who believe candy is the best solution for a tantrum and that a nice home-cooked meal brings harmony to the home. It is a universally acknowledged fact that mothers overcompensate. Working moms certainly do. There is a tendency for most new mothers to pander to their families and ignore their faults when they cannot give enough time to them. However, as time passes, you'll realise lollipops aren't the solution to long-term happiness. Communication is. Start learning to forgive your maternal misgivings and grow from your mistakes right now.

When it comes to family, mothers should avoid expecting much from others and instead be grateful for any help they can get. Communicating with partners and family about their expectations is a must. Your partner will not magically know you're having a hard time if you don't talk to them about it.

Verbalising the request can help you more than you realise. Don't expect people to understand your cry for help when you haven't been speaking up about it. Similarly, don't expect them to always be ready at your beck and call. Your child and home are your responsibility, not theirs. Whatever help you get, be grateful and appreciative for it.

This line of thought can also extend to your partner/ husband as well. If your partner is willing to help out even when you haven't asked them to, take the help and appreciate it. At the same time, if your partner does not have enough time or isn't ready to help, shake the negativity off. Situations like these can add a toxic edge to your relationship, especially if the other person cannot meet your expectations like you want them to. Don't let this become an underlying issue.

Instead, take control of the situation and find alternative help for additional support. You could always get domestic help for household assistance or find daycares for your children while at work. There's a workable solution for your troubles out there, as long as you keep looking out for one. When you allow other people to control your expectations, you set yourself up for disappointment. So, take charge of your own happiness and move forth.

## The 'Let It Go' Philosophy

I never expected the most revolutionary, life-changing motherhood advice I'd ever get to come from a Disney movie. Are you worried that your child had a tumble or skipped a meal? Let it go. Are you feeling guilty that you bought fast food for dinner instead of cooking at home? Let it go. It's completely normal for your child and you to make mistakes. Please don't take it personally as to how good a mother you are.

My son went through a phase of not eating solid food for quite some time. He would only eat fruits. Slowly, he started to develop a taste for solid food as time went by. As a mother, I could have panicked about his eating habits and rushed him to doctors to figure out what was wrong. I didn't. Instead, I let it go. I knew that if I pushed him to change his eating habits, he would get uncomfortable and not react well to me forcing him. My son loves all his solids now, and he would have definitely developed a complex towards them if I had forced them onto him earlier.

This philosophy can be applied to your relationship with your partner as well. Don't make anyone do things they don't want to. It just creates negativity in the relationship. If you expect and demand their help at home, it will backfire on you. Indian men, in particular, are notoriously clueless about how to help out, not because they don't want to, but simply because they've never been taught to. Their fathers, uncles, grandfathers, etc., were never expected to be involved in roles beyond being head of the household, and they internalised those thought processes. Rather than demanding help, let them organically learn as time goes on. You will be surprised how quickly people grow out of their quirks if you don't force their hand.

## The Definition of a Good Mother

Conventional society dictates that a good mother is one who thrives on all aspects of motherhood. Everyone paints a very rosy picture of what motherhood should be. Women love talking about how being a mother is the most fulfilling feeling on Earth.

Let's normalise mothers that don't always feel like being a mother is the best feeling they've ever experienced. That happiness is an on-and-off feeling. When we pressure mothers to feel a certain way, we marginalise many of them in the process. It is okay to have mixed emotions and completely normal to feel not good about being a mother in terms of expectations from yourself.

After birth, all mothers can attest that every nerve ending in their being feels like a raw burst of emotion. You have a large stomach, you've put on a lot of weight, you're constantly leaking at the breasts, and on top of everything, a little baby who depends on you for everything. It is a very different feeling, and it can be incredibly overwhelming.

We've all heard that seeing your baby after birth is the best feeling on the planet. And it is. But it is all equally terrifying to look down at your body and see blood everywhere. When you see yourself like that, it's enough to make anyone feel vulnerable and scared. So, when people around you constantly remind you of how happy you should be, it makes you feel guilty.

It's alright if you aren't feeling enlightened as a mother when you see yourself like that.

Remember, everyone has their own definition of what being a good mother entails. Personally, I don't think there are any right or wrong ways you can be a mother. Everyone does it their way. When it comes to raising their kids, some people prefer a methodological approach prescribed by doctors or books, and others have more of an instinctual approach to motherhood. I'm more of an intuitive mom myself. If I had to give my readers some advice, it would only be this. ALL MOTHERS ARE GOOD MOTHERS. Do what feels natural to you, and trust your gut above anything else. A mother's instinct is a powerful thing. Most importantly, don't let a stranger's unsolicited advice dictate your emotions.

## Motherhood is a Bumpy Ride

I am a brutally honest person and don't enjoy sugar-coating reality just for the sake of others. That emotional stability has guided the way I approach motherhood as well. I knew that being a mother would be an emotionally bumpy journey for me from the very beginning. There are days when I feel on top of the world as a mom. Similarly, there are others where I feel the complete opposite.

I don't subscribe to the thought of putting mothers on pedestals. In fact, I think it limits them from realising their full potential. The first six weeks after my delivery, I was a bundle of frenetic energy. So much so that I was rushing my son around with me to work and other activities as soon as I could. I didn't want to focus on the positive and negative energy brewing inside me. Instead, I channelled all of it into productive output.

People forget that being a mother and realising the stressors that come with it are old-school problems. Instead of letting them bog us down, we need to start working around them. My go-to method was channelling that mixed bag of emotion into a singular focus. It can be different for different people.

If you are emotional and prefer talking to people to understand your vulnerable thoughts and other things in your mind, do that. Whatever works for you. Speak to your family, friends, gynaecologist, lactation specialist, psychiatrist, absolutely anyone who you can safely go to and share opinions, feelings, and doubts. It's okay to say that you don't feel good about yourself on some days. It's fine not to want to feed the baby on a particular day. Just remember that it's normal to feel these emotions, and it is important to vocalise your feelings instead of keeping them to yourself.

I encourage mothers to extend this approach towards motherhood to other facets of their lives as well. Trust your intuition, and don't pressurise yourself to fit society's mould of what a 'perfect mother' is. There is no right path to motherhood. Most importantly, stop comparing yourself to others. Stop comparing your child to other children. Kids grow at their own pace and will reach their necessary developmental milestones when they are ready to. Instead, focus on the incredible journey that motherhood continues to be for your child and you.

## Dealing with Expectations

Mothers have a tough time letting go of the stress that comes with expectations. We're practically and biologically hardwired to live a life of stress as soon as we become mothers. I've always been the kind of person that stays calm under pressure. However, there have been moments in my life when I have become overwrought with stress. Just last week, my son fell off a chair while playing and ended up bleeding out of his ear. The sight of blood set off panic alarms within me I didn't even know existed. Thankfully, my husband and I rushed him to the hospital as fast as possible and confirmed it to be a minor injury.

En route to the hospital, my husband tried to distract me from my fear by telling me he never expected me to panic this much. But seeing my son in pain for the first time in forever caused me to instinctually panic like never before.

My husband's words helped me realise a few things. I needed to let go of the stress I was feeling. We were lucky that this was the first time our son had had a serious fall in six years. My fellow moms know that kids have an endless supply of energy for shenanigans that can result in all sorts of bumps and bruises. Fortunately for me, my child's naughty side has not been extreme or gotten him into any major mishaps. I choose to be grateful for that instead.

Your mindset can change if you learn to approach challenging situations through mindfulness. Meditation and yoga have really helped centre me and given me complete clarity regarding such feelings. Just ten minutes of yoga and meditation a day can really help in keeping you calm and give you the power to let go. These mindfulness practices have helped me at work too. When I'm facing a particularly stressful day at work, I take five deep breaths and allow myself to let go of the negativity surrounding me.

As a rule of thumb, remember this - you cannot change or control the people or situations around you. The only thing you can do is control the tidal wave of reactive emotion within you by choosing not to react to them and letting go of any negative feelings you feel.

## Make Mindfulness a Mindset

Remember, me-time is essential for increasing meditative focus and overall mindful living. You don't always need anyone around you; sometimes, you need to be alone with your thoughts. So go out for a long walk with your earphones in, paint – any time you choose to consciously reconnect with yourself, you are loving yourself. You cannot truly love anyone else without loving yourself. For example, if spending time with friends, making dance videos, or getting dressed up to go out makes you happy, do it.

# 3

# Moms Vs Change

As a mom sipping her cup of morning coffee with her child running around the house, I think it's fair to say that motherhood changes a woman. My nights used to involve martinis, stilettos, and little black dresses, but nowadays, most nights are spent singing Baby Shark on repeat and sleeping at 9 p.m. The stark difference between life then and now can overwhelm many, but here's a newsflash: it's not all that bad.

The honest to God truth is that the changes brought on by becoming a newlywed bride were far more brutal for me than the changes I faced pre-and post- the birth of my child. I got married fairly young, at 23. It was quite a whirlwind wedding, despite us having dated for one and a half years before getting married!

Comparatively, my pregnancy journey was a smooth ride. No, seriously, it was a blast. I had absolutely no bad days and not even a little bit of morning sickness or nausea. Instead, all I remember is being a force of turbulent energy for nine months and going on a desert safari in Dubai, flying from Kuala Lumpur to Kolkata while 7 months pregnant to set up an office there, etc. But, of course, it might have been because my pregnancy was planned, and I knew what to expect.

More than the pregnancy itself, the people around me helped shape a lot of changes within me. The support around oneself, including family, doctors, and other medical professionals, is powerful for a mother's well-being. My gynaecologists in Kolkata and Kuala Lumpur, respectively, were massively supportive of me trying new things during the pregnancy and dissuaded any fears I might have had. They told me I could do anything short of bungee jumping off a plane, as long as I was comfortable doing it.

Since then, I think I have become a lot calmer. I have also gotten a lot more patient with life. But, for my unwed child free readers, here's a little secret. If you thought you were a patient person now, wait till after you get married and have children. If changing nappies and putting down the toilet seat for the millionth time teaches you anything in life, it's that enlightenment and patience are virtues only wives and mothers can fully grasp!

## The Story of My Pregnancy

I've gone into just a little bit of detail before, but here's the complete story. People say a mother experiences a rush of love like never before when she holds her baby for the first time. But, for me, it was not quite like that. I first felt that rush of love on 23 January 2015. It was the day after my birthday, and I had recently taken a positive home pregnancy test. So, after confiding in a friend on my birthday, I was told to see a gynaecologist to confirm my pregnancy and get everything checked out. At the gynaecologist's chamber, after confirming everything was alright, I was asked whether I wanted to hear my baby's heartbeat or not. I kid you not, the moment I listened to my child's heartbeat, the world seemed to stop, and I had tears falling down my eyes. It was at that moment I fell in love with my baby for the first time.

My pregnancy was very smooth, but the moment Aryan was born, things weren't. I remember everything like it happened just yesterday. I had just eaten *paani puri* (a popular Indian street food) before reaching the hospital and was looking forward to seeing my baby boy. The delivery went well, but soon after, I was told that Aryan had faced some complications during the birth and was put into the NICU for two weeks. After that, everything seemed to change in a matter of seconds.

The first time I saw my son, he was tucked into a cot in the NICU, a glass window separating us. Seeing him with wires all over was heartbreaking. I hadn't expected to be separated from my son after such an easy pregnancy. That was a traumatising week for me. Even until very recently, whenever I spoke about this incident, I used to get deeply emotional.

I don't think I shed a single tear until the night before I was to be discharged from the hospital, knowing he wasn't going to go back home with me. Of course, my whole family had cried at one point or another, but I knew I had to stay strong for Aryan and myself. So, when my husband walked in on my crying that night, he held me close and said, "Shikha, I haven't been able to cry all this time because you have been so strong." Knowing my sadness was shared helped me get through that rough time much quicker.

After marriage, your life changes a lot. But pregnancy is an entirely different journey altogether. I was suddenly aware that I was now responsible for the new life I had given birth to and his well-being. The protective mom instinct in me was at an all-time high after my son was born. However, I made sure I came out of that as soon as possible. I refused to ponder how difficult it had all been because that would have been an extremely unhealthy mindset to live with. Instead, I chose to deal with anything the world has thrown at me as it comes, as I did not want my son to grow up fearful because that would mean I was doing him a big disservice as his mom.

**Navigating Work Culture after Becoming a Mother**

Before Aryan was born, I mainly worked as a consultant in the events industry. The kind of work that kept me busy at all times of the day and night. But after I found out I was expecting, I knew I wanted to make some lifestyle changes and stick to a profession that doesn't call for obnoxious working hours, thus prompting the restart of my venture into digital marketing.

I am of the personal belief that children cannot express themselves emotionally and verbally until they're two years old. So, until Aryan was 2 years old, I tried to be with him as much as I could. It was only after that I got him to a Montessori cum day-care.

The issue that remained was that until then, he was a newborn and newborns can't communicate all that well. You can expect them to cry at the most unexpected or undesired times. As mothers, we are hardwired to become conscious and uncomfortable with that behaviour, and it is tricky to navigate client meetings and work because of it. Not going to lie, I, too, initially felt embarrassed because my son cried during work and meetings.

However, I soon realised that it is always good to be candid about such matters. Indra Nooyi once said that you need to create an ecosystem around your work, where, if need be, your colleagues, clients, etc., can chip in to help whenever you need them. That worked for me. People appreciate honesty. Be open about your motherhood journey and let them know that your baby might be heard during the call. As long as you are fully committed to everything you do, no one will ever begrudge you for it. I had something to prove to people who thought mothers in business could not fully perform their jobs, so I worked hard to dissuade them from that stereotype.

I used to work as a consultant for a company that had recently employed a then 6-month pregnant lady. A surprising move, considering how much bias mothers face in a professional workspace. That co-worker was a force of nature for me. You see, in Malaysia, you get two months of maternity leave and have the choice to take it either before or after the birth of your baby. She decided she'd use all her time off after the baby was born and was extremely disciplined at work. So much so that she came in even on the day of her delivery. I had to literally push her out of the office and convince her to have the baby! The positive energy I got from seeing her attitude was everything. My co-worker inspired me to work till the ninth month of my pregnancy too. It's amazing what one can achieve through the right inspiration.

I'm incredibly proud of the hurdles I have overcome during my journey thereafter. Being a mother has not slowed me down at all. On the contrary, my career has boomed in the last six years and continues to grow with time.

## Change From Within: The Myth of the Perfect Mother

The biggest lie mothers tell themselves is that being a mom doesn't leave them with enough time to do other things, i.e., the things they want. This is not true (AT ALL). Being a mother has not kept me from doing the things I wanted to do. If anything, motherhood has made me feel like I am Shikha version 2.0! I've travelled the most I ever have with my infant son and am so much more confident in how I live my life now.

Don't let others around you define your life, telling you that you cannot reach for the stars because you are a mother. If you let motherhood become an excuse for you to remain regretful, you're doing yourself a massive disservice. Compromise is part and parcel of life, and you will have to make allowances for specific events/situations. However, if something truly matters to you, go for it. Do not let yourself miss out on opportunities because you are a mother.

I make it a point to achieve at least two new goals every single year to keep myself growing. Last year, I became a certified underwater diver. I needed to be in the water with a massive oxygen tank for more than three hours every day to get the certification. Instead of using my son as an excuse to not be able to do what I wanted to, I found an alternative where my husband took care of our son during that week.

If being a perfect mom is making you unhappy, be an imperfect one! You're still a good mom, no matter what. In the past, my mother would often tell me that my sister is such a hands-on mom because she took time to make laddus and fresh vegetable soup for her baby for snacks. I would nod sagely and agree with everything she said while giving Aryan cookies (the kind that came from a box). The truth is, there are lots of moms out there who love taking the time and effort to make snacks from scratch for their children, and at the same time, there are others that think that gluten-free oat cookies from the store work just as well.

I have always been clear about how I didn't want to be one of those mothers who makes their entire life about their children and then wonder where their entire lives have gone. You cannot compromise on your own life just because you are a mother now. Other than a mother, I am also a woman, a wife, and a girl who has her own dreams. We sometimes tend to forget that our whole identity is not one of a mother's. We have a lot of other roles to play in life.

## A Change to Embrace: The Post Baby Body

When I got pregnant, I had a vision of how I'd look as a mom-to-be. The image included a perfectly rounded belly and a face that was almost always glowing. So, when I got perpetually swollen feet, sore breasts, and tiger stripes instead, it took me a while to get used to it. We're all programmed by the media to think of pregnant women as regular women but with strategically placed baby bumps.

Self-acceptance, especially for mothers, can be polarising. On the one hand, women are lauded for being mothers while also being body shamed for not bouncing back fast enough. Sameera Reddy said it best when she called out the 'ideal' vision of motherhood perpetuated by the media and the 'yummy mummy' storyline the glamorous film industry she worked in had set.

Luckily for me, I have a very supportive partner in my husband, who helped me let go of my insecurities during pregnancy. Even my parents and in-laws were incredibly supportive! Today, women are controlling the narrative. Social media sites like Instagram and Facebook have started to become safe spaces for women by allowing them to celebrate their pregnant bodies. We see so many fabulous mothers who show off their unedited baby bumps and have glamorous photoshoots that document their motherhood journey, setting realistic goals for so many moms out there!

Gone are the days of magazines showering celebrity moms with love because they reached their pre-pregnancy weight so quickly. They have fancy personal trainers and maybe excellent genes that help them get into that shape! Most women don't. Most of us will always have stretch marks that remind us of how strong we were and a certain amount of softness to our bodies that will never really go away. So, let's embrace that instead!

Do you want to wear a bikini on your next beach vacation? Go for it! When you feel confident about your body, you feel good about yourself. We live in an era where real women are unapologetically sharing their real-life experiences and bodies, fighting the age-old narrative that brands marketing the 'right' body have set. So, let's celebrate that and set better examples that inspire more women in the future.

## Prioritise Your Partner

Bringing children into the family dynamic does change it, but always for the better. I believe children strengthen the bond between partners and enrich the relationship's aura by adding a new dimension to it. However, having one-on-one time with your spouse/partner is still incredibly important. My husband and I make it a point to do regular couple activities together, like, movie nights, dinners, etc. and, just in general, spend time together as a couple.

# 4

# Moms Vs Communication

This chapter is specifically for the readers that have panic attacks or dramatically faint at the thought of calling someone and asking for help. Which, surprise, surprise, is a lot of you. Independent Woman by Destiny's Child might be the soundtrack you wanted for your life, but the harsh reality is that you aren't Beyoncé, and your life isn't as breezy as you want it to be.

If you ask me, most women are too proud to ask for help, which is why they cannot communicate their needs properly. Asking for help doesn't mean you are weak or incapable of doing things yourself; it just means you have other commitments that need your attention more.

If you don't want to ask someone for help because of a rocky relationship, you are well within your means to do so. But if you're not asking for help because of your pride or another's assumed judgement, then you are in the wrong.

Let's take family, for instance. It should be easy to ask for help from family. However, I have met many women who don't like asking for help from their moms-in-law because they don't want them to assume that they are constantly asking for favours from them, cannot handle responsibilities, etc. Personally, I don't feel that way. Then again, everyone has different family dynamics, and one cannot judge them without really knowing what kind of relationship they share with someone. If I'm not on good terms with someone, even I'd be apprehensive about asking them for help.

In the past, we have seen our mothers and grandmothers handle things at home so seamlessly that we think we can do it ourselves, too, not realising that effortlessness was the effort of everyone chipping in to help with the family, home, and children. When we assume we can handle everything without asking for help, we convince ourselves we don't need it, creating an unhealthy and toxic edge to our lives.

I've always been open when it comes to asking for help. It takes a village to raise a child, and I believe all mothers need a positive ecosystem around them to make it work. Fostering those relationships at work and with friends and family takes time and effort but is worth it in the end.

## There's always help if You need it

As a self-employed mother, I agree I have a certain amount of privilege when it comes to taking care of my child. I am able to take my son along with me whenever required, so I can sympathise when I see other women talk about how stressful and difficult things can be. But only to a certain extent.

In a world where day-care services are so readily available, stop complaining and start communicating your need for help. The option to ask your neighbours for help, since most of us live in condos and societies nowadays, also exists. Even stay at home moms have started to send their kids to daycares. Maybe the point of it is to help the child socialise better, but I think it is fascinating that asking for help is not limited, or only taboo, to working mothers.

If the person you are requesting loves your child and takes your request in a positive way, then there's no harm in asking for help. Whenever I am back home in Kolkata, I hardly get to see my son. He's always either with my mother or mother-in-law, but he's never with me. In-office, he's with an office colleague.

Children are positively affected by instances that allow them to socialise with others. As most families now have one child, they enjoy any moment when they can make a new friend or have someone to play with.

## Are You asking, or are You demanding help?

Mothers that expect and demand help whenever they need it make me cringe. When it comes to communication, you are setting yourself up for disappointment if you expect the people around you to help you without any questions. The thing is, if you're staying with family, you can expect their help if required because families work on the principles of unconditional love and reciprocity.

But when you, like me, live in a country where your friends are your chosen family and most significant support, you can't. When your friends, family, and colleagues do things for you, it comes from a place of pure love and is not a situation where you demand it, whenever you want.

The other day, I had a vaccine appointment and had taken my son along with me. It was a little stressful keeping an eye out for him and getting the jab simultaneously. Afterwards, I went to a friend's house to talk and catch up. When I told her about how I took Aryan with me for my vaccine appointment, she got so angry! She asked me why didn't I just leave him with her. I was touched by her warmth and realised she was right.

Her emotions made me feel how fortunate I was. It was out of pure love that she demanded why I didn't leave Aryan with her. Moments like that cement lifelong bonds, and if you have that kind of relationship with a person, you should always take help from them if need be. You don't always have to take the onus on yourself and can take time off if you really need to, without judgement.

## Making Communication a Judgement Free Zone

Effective communication can be summed up in two words: mutual and balanced. For example, when my friend asked me why I didn't leave my son with her while getting vaccinated, she did it out of love. That love was strengthened by the fact that we have always helped each other out whenever required.

When I bring Aryan to the office, my colleagues genuinely love talking and spending time with him. If they brought their children to work, I would do the same thing. Any situation that demands help needs to be based on the principle of pure love. If anybody feels like they are being used while helping out, then that relationship can be considered irrevocably damaged.

Communication regarding the care of your child requires being able to walk a very fine, balanced line. So, when you are asking your family or friends for help, let that request come from a genuine place. I have been very blessed in this aspect; my husband and I don't even have to ask family for help when we go visit them. My parents and in-laws actually argue about where Aryan will stay when we go to visit them in Kolkata. The fathers literally quarrel and make elaborate plans over phone calls to get equal time with their grandchild. That, too, is because of mutual love and respect between us.

If you think someone is not happy to take care of your child, don't leave your child with that person. That would be a clear example of a no-no situation, if there were any. If there is even the slightest bit of negativity or resentment there, you cannot trust your child with that person.

Women who judge other women are a big part of the problem. If I could, I'd rather pretend these women didn't exist as they give mothers everywhere a bad name. Dealing with women like this boils down to not reacting or responding to their verbal bile. I didn't sign up to be part of Modi Ji's Swachh Bharat Abhiyan, so I don't concern myself with trash.

If someone judges you for small things like having domestic help or dropping your kids late to school, it is their problem and their problem alone. Envious people show their true colours by pretending to be moralistic and using that superiority complex to put people down. If putting people down makes them feel happy, then that says a lot more about their lives and personalities than it does about my shortcomings.

In a recent conversation with a friend, she told me that sometimes women who have achieved lesser than you want to utter such words to please their ego. If this is what makes them happy, so be it. Instead, choose not to get affected by such toxic comments.

## Your in-laws are not the Enemy

A common trope in family-centric movies and TV shows worldwide is having a toxic, up to nothing good, meddling mother-in-law. Most times, that mother-in-law wears dark makeup and considers the daughter-in-law to be the enemy trying to steal her precious baby boy (who is actually a full-grown man!). Unfortunately, it's a very stereotypically Indian phenomenon to internalise this fact. As a result, brides are often warned to remain wary of their in-laws.

Through years of observation, I've come to realise that most women initially assume that their mothers-in-law are the devil incarnate and will forever remain a thorn in their sides, despite it not actually being true. To have an unfounded bias against your in-laws is a toxic trait. They are a part of your family, and your kids are their grandkids. That relationship is a real and valid one, despite whatever assumptions you have about them.

I've written about the importance of maintaining a positive ecosystem around oneself earlier on. Dealing with family can be stressful if not done well; however, you can maintain favourable relationships with them if you can avoid being reactive to everything they do/say in the heat of the moment. Understanding your in-laws' perspectives and mindsets is one of the best ways you can foster a warm and loving relationship with them.

## Communication and Mutual Respect

Let's say you have a close friend who taught your children to cuss when you left them in his charge. Or family members who give your children candy and chocolates close to their bedtime, making it impossible for you to get them to sleep on time. How do you lay down specific rules and conditions with friends and family when you are the one asking for help?

Asking people not to undermine your parental decisions is a difficult conversation to have. Some people assume that offering help with childcare gives them the license to parent as well. But unfortunately, there is no easy way to deal with situations like these. It all depends on who you are dealing with. If it is an older person, you might want to explore whether there is a grain of wisdom in what they said. If not, laugh off their suggestions politely.

You will be at an impasse if you try to fight their mindset by arguing the point they are making. When an older person takes time to teach or explain things to someone, they genuinely believe they're doing and saying something right and wise. If that advice comes from a space of love, affection, and care, accept it humbly or ignore it completely. It is not always necessary to put your foot down and make a scene about things.

When you leave your child with someone, let them take care of the child as best they can, using whatever methods they feel are best. Do not start putting conditions and rules on that care and expect people to follow your way of parenting, especially when you have requested them to care for your child.

If something they do makes you extremely uncomfortable, then put it across to them softly. Use phrases like 'I would prefer it if you could…', etc., while making your point, and always make sure that you respect their feelings.

However, if someone I know purposely breaks my trust by not taking care of my child properly, I would consider it a breach of trust and never try to seek them out again. Communication, especially with regard to parenting, is about mutual trust. These conversations need to be about more than ego, and genuine love between all parties is essential.

## Respect Caregivers' Feelings

To effectively communicate with loved ones, you need to start by respecting their feelings. Just like you are a mother learning to take care of your child, they too are dealing with the addition of a new member of the family. Respect that they are trying their hardest.

You shouldn't be treating your family like domestic help or a free daycare service. If you don't like something they did, learn to ignore it or figure out a way to communicate your worries gently and mindfully. Don't bark orders at them, and respect whatever assistance they are providing you. If you're asking for help, then you need to learn to accept their caregiving ideologies.

# 5

# Moms Vs Identity Crises

*"I can't think
of any better representation of beauty than
someone who is unafraid to be herself."*
**– Emma Stone –**

I went out shopping at the mall yesterday and, surprisingly enough, ran into one of my son's teachers there. To be polite, I went to greet her, only for her to look at me with furrowed brows. I had met her at his school just the previous week, yet she seemed to genuinely have no idea who I was. Other people may have gotten offended at this point, but I knew exactly what the issue was. So, I reintroduced myself. "Hi, I'm Shikha, Aryan's mom." That was when recognition struck her!

The reality is that most women's identity, after giving birth, becomes an extension of their child. I still introduce myself as 'Aryan's mom' to fellow daycare parents rather than by my name! Most people assume that post motherhood, a woman's life and general purpose will revolve solely around her family's wellbeing and welfare. But that's not true. She needs to make herself a priority. A mother's happiness is paramount for her family's overall wellness.

Personally, I have tried to maintain my identity as a woman and as a mother very separately because I believe that taking time for myself is a form of therapy. I don't forgo lunches with my girls, spa days, etc., and am okay not feeling guilty leaving my son with my husband if I need a night out once a month. It's perfectly fine (and normal!) to do that.

When we shame mothers by trying to fit them into a typecast mould, we do them an enormous injustice. Choosing whether you are a woman or a mother isn't an either/or situation. The precise art of balancing these two roles is how a mother can realign her identity and confidence with who she used to be.

## Children and Identity Crisis

Last week, my five-year-old son was caught trying to fry an egg for himself. My husband was about to head out for work when he saw Aryan holding an egg and taking determined steps towards the kitchen. The reason? He wanted to show his mom he was self-sufficient and didn't want to disturb her during her work meeting. That's when I knew I was doing a good job raising my son. It made me realise that children can learn to be independent through experiences like this. Unfortunately, it is very common to see mothers, especially Indian mothers, falling over backwards to meet the needs and demands of their children.

I think it is of utmost importance to align your kids to your lifestyle rather than always trying to fit into their schedules. I have friends who are challenging to make plans with because they are constantly trying to revolve their lives around their children, not giving attention or importance to the way they want to live their own lives.

I think it should be the other way around. Children are very open to behavioural changes and can be taught to understand certain truths very early. I had mentioned before that because I travelled a lot with my son from when he was a toddler, he learnt to be an excellent instinctual traveller from the beginning. It is not easy for mothers to travel with their toddlers, yet he accompanied me to almost six wonders of the world before he was 3 years old. Try to mould your kids to fit into your routine, and not vice versa, so you don't end up losing your identity for the sake of your child.

When people raise their kids with certain ideals and reinforce them from early childhood, it helps them handle certain expectations calmly. Your kids should not take you for granted and must know that their mothers will not always be available at their disposal. Children need to know that you, as a parent, have an identity outside of them and that you cannot adjust your time according to their schedule.

When you pander to your children, you begin to lose your identity as a woman. If you set yourself up to conform to societal expectations of a good mom, you are setting yourself up for failure because you cannot live up to those impossible standards. Trying to fit an ideal will only make you diminish yourself in the process, causing you to remain largely unfulfilled and unhappy.

## Motherhood is not an Excuse

Birth and motherhood do bring changes, but that doesn't mean it can't all work out wonderfully. It's a process that doesn't happen in a day, and you will need to accommodate the changes that come your way. However, as time goes by, you can successfully learn to fit your child into the schedule that will eventually come about with your work and other priorities in life.

It goes without saying that being a mom is one's main priority after becoming a mother. But it doesn't mean that there isn't anything else they can do. Sometimes, in the process of being a mother, we forget that our children are our first priorities, not our only ones.

To use your child as a bargaining chip for your forgotten dreams is a poor excuse. Modern society glorifies stay-at-home mothers even today, despite the fact that a lot of women choose to work after childbirth. Praise is a double-edged sword that can make people struggle with their identity. On the one hand, people tell mothers that they must care for their children but then switch the narrative by telling them they are wasting their lives and potential.

This is why I have certain reservations about whether being a stay-at-home mom is ideal for women. Unless a stay-at-home mother actively pursues other interests, she will fall into a deep cycle of resentment. For example, one of my friends, a stay-at-home mom, always feels the need to introduce herself by saying that she used to be an architect but is currently a stay-at-home mom. She even started a YouTube channel, so she doesn't come up empty-handed when people ask her what she does.

So, why does she feel the need to defend herself against judgement? Because while we glorify homemakers, we don't give them due respect in society. I believe that if women can invest so much time, effort, and money into their education and career, then they deserve to not give up on it and further their lives by bettering themselves.

## Society and Identity Crisis

If you have ever glimpsed one of the many matrimonial advertisements in Indian newspapers, you are in for a treat. The requirements for potential brides include everything from a suggested skin colour (the lighter, the better), schooling (at least Harvard educated), to whether they can scale the Swiss Alps! It goes without saying that one of the most significant stakeholders when it comes to a woman's identity is the society she lives in. Since I come from the Kolkata Marwari scene, let's talk about that. The culture I come from is still highly orthodox, and we often see parents sending their daughters to universities abroad to study, only to get them married soon after and have a "settled life."

Recently, a case garnered massive traction in the news involving a young woman who killed herself due to the abuse she allegedly faced at the hands of her husband and in-laws. This girl belonged to an uber-rich family and had a stellar academic background. But unfortunately, her father pushed her to marry as soon as she graduated from university, and despite her hesitations, he married her off to what he considered a 'good family'. While he was not directly responsible for the abuse she faced, he was partially to be blamed for the tragic decision she took later. The toxic societal setup might have been why she died, but her nearest and dearest failed her in equal measure.

I remember my mother telling me that she had once excitedly gotten college admission forms home, only to have her mother rip them up soon after. The reason: she didn't think my mother needed to be more educated. This is not an example from a bygone era. The reality is that women are still vilified for being 'too' anything. Being too educated, too opinionated, and too ambitious is, to this day, considered a negative attribute. Similarly, I have had female friends whose in-laws show off their degrees and education like badges of honour, only to expect them to cook food and wash the dishes at home.

This hypocrisy within society can cause a woman to have an identity crisis; women themselves are complicit in this, though — they can have an identity crisis by remaining in a comfort zone that's toxic for their wellbeing.

Likewise, I would be remiss if I didn't mention the obsession with changing bodies here. Society and media tell us that being a mother is beautiful, but in the same vein, they sell us propaganda that makes us feel awful about the way we look. So, let's normalise mom bodies!

I think there's something extraordinary about the maternity journey. Sure, your body changes and your breasts and vagina feel like they belong to a different person, but you have a beautiful child in the end. That unbreakable bond you created is worth everything.

There's very little discourse on this publicly, and we need to educate more women on how normal it is. Of course, only a select few ever really go back to their pre-baby body, but most women just need to accept that their new body is their forever one. They will always have a softness to their body, regardless of how much they exercise. If we can age gracefully, why can't we love our changing bodies gracefully as well?

## Realigning Your Current Identity with Your Past

I am sure a rare breed of women exists out there who, after giving birth, just looked in the mirror and decreed themselves perfect. I wish I was one of them, but making peace with the fact that I am a whole new person with very different priorities was difficult.

Have you noticed that most people don't like talking about the challenges that come with motherhood?

This is because we are all fed the narrative that motherhood cannot be anything other than idyllic. As a result, no one really talks about how motherhood is a journey that redefines you at your very core.

Learning to realign who you are with who you were is difficult. I wish I had someone who told me that I would not have good days all the time but that I could enjoy my journey as a mom as long as I did everything at my own pace. If I had to give you the one piece of advice that helped me immensely, it would be this: Accept your circumstances. At any given point in time, you need to make peace with that fact.

Your previous goals and ambitions haven't come to a complete standstill after the birth of your child. You can still have everything you ever wanted, just in due course and not all at once. All you need to do is continue working on yourself. For example, you could start by listing out the top ten things you consider essential to your wellbeing. The list could include anything from having a career, vacations, meeting your friends, regular date nights, etc.

Once you have a list ready, please make it a point to prioritise them in your life and adjust your routine and childcare schedule accordingly. If you don't give yourself importance, you will never be truly happy and will always curse the life you have chosen for yourself. So, try to make the things on your list a priority.

In my case, I made sure I took time off to do the things I loved to do. So, if I wanted to try out a new restaurant with my girlfriends, I'd plan ahead of time and circle the dates in both my husband's and my calendars. Even if my husband had last-minute work coming up, I made sure he knew my plans were a priority. There might have been a brief period of adjustment, but it all worked out in the end. The fact that all things have a way of working out is advice everyone gives, but no one takes to heart. Becoming a mother is reaching a pitstop in your life, not one that diminishes you, but one that transforms you for the better.

## Your Sense of Self Depends on You

Think back to when you got your first pay cheque or when you finally managed to potty train your child successfully. These achievements, big or small, made you feel good about yourself, didn't they? I think it goes without saying that self-worth, self-confidence, and feelings of accomplishment are of utmost importance to a person's overall happiness.

Mothers need to invest time in activities that make their self-worth bloom. Planning ahead of time and making yourself a priority is the key to successfully navigating the topsy turvy life that motherhood is synonymous with.

Women, at their core, have always required balance to thrive in life. Men can still get away with being single-minded in their pursuits, but women have always been expected to handle all responsibilities given to them since time immemorial. From keeping families from falling apart to maintaining relationships, a mother's life is a delicate balancing act at its core. Prioritising your needs through actions and affirmations can help maintain that balance easier.

If you struggle with prioritising yourself over your child, ask yourself this – you compartmentalise everything in your life. Your career is tailored to meet your needs, not the other way around. So why can't you learn to balance your child's routine in a way that seamlessly transitions into your own? The best thing moms today can do is learn to balance their child's needs with what they want to do in life.

## Learn a New Skill Every Year

Every woman's priority should be acquiring a new skill every year. It helps with building their identity and confidence. Something like going for a public speaking engagement, learning a new language, etc., are all skills that can be developed sitting at home, at the pace you want to go! If you really want to do something, no excuses can stop you from going for it. The output depends entirely on how much time, effort, and passion you want to contribute to the cause.

You need to aim for the moon; only then will you land among the stars. Even if you try hard and fail, you'll be in a better place than where you started off. Acquiring a new skill set doesn't always involve taking big actions; even the most minor things can transform you.

6

# Moms Vs The Supermom Paradox

I think my son is convinced that I am a superhero. He was watching cartoons the other day, and as soon as some Wonder Woman-esque heroine saved the day, he looked at me and smiled, 'Like mama!"

I am glad my son thinks I am hiding a red cape in my closet, even if, according to him, a superhero is someone who makes pancakes every Sunday morning. All good superheroes have a tragic origin story that gives them substance, and you know what, so do all mothers.

Life after giving birth for most women is a series of ups and downs. Some face lows like never before, and others take to motherhood like fish to water. Many of us might not have actually heard anyone around us use the words postpartum depression or baby blues very much, but thanks to social media, we've all become more attuned to the struggles others face. I, for one, am glad that things that were considered taboo to talk about are being brought to the frontline.

The lows can come in the form of many things: how your body is acting, lowered self-esteem, etc. For example, after birth, a woman's body goes haywire, literally. You have stretch marks all over; you get acne, your hair starts to fall, it can be a lot for anyone to go through, and you suddenly begin to feel a lot older than you are. I think all mothers go through a little bit of baby blues for that very reason — another reason could be that some women struggle with how to be mothers.

The journey of motherhood is relatively easier when you are pregnant. If you take good care of yourself, you will ultimately take good care of your baby as well. But once the baby is born, the dynamics change completely. When you're dealing with your body insecurities and adding a baby's wellbeing – vaccinations, sickness etc., on top of it, it is easy to get overwhelmed.

That's why they say a woman is reborn after giving birth. While all of us go through changes pre and post-birth, the magnitude with which they affect us is different. Your pregnancy journey will either leave you feeling less confident with lower self-esteem, or you will feel liberated knowing you are a changed woman with a new lease on life and your body.

## Motherhood: The Most Beautiful Feeling on Earth

It is hard to believe that people didn't know what the word 'depression' meant just a few short years ago. Then, most people thought that it was slang for being an extremely negative person. So, when topics like postpartum depression were discussed, they were misunderstood or cast aside as irrelevant. After all, how can one be depressed even after going through the most beautiful feeling on earth, 'motherhood'?

Facts like this are why I am reminded that the Internet always does more good than harm.

Ever since the conversation about these topics started, people have begun to share their own experiences as well. With that taboo broken, it is becoming increasingly normal for mothers to talk about feeling low about their bodies, themselves, and the new life role they are starting.

Motherhood is an entire lifestyle overhaul, and it is difficult to get used to. Post-baby blues is not only about the baby but the fact that the whole setup around you has changed radically. Before becoming a mother, you were your biggest priority, and now, the little bundle in your arms is. Where you were once independent and fancy-free, now you rush basic activities like using the loo because someone very vulnerable out there is waiting for you. It can take up to a week to plan a simple brunch out. You don't do anything impulsive anymore unless impulsive means picking up ice cream on the way back home from school.

I think every woman goes through a little bit of an emotional slump post-birth, and it was true for me as well. I am a very strong headed person by nature, but not being able to hold my son after his birth nearly broke me. My son was born on 15th September 2015, and it was only a week later that I was allowed to feed him directly for the first time, just to see if he could latch properly. It might sound very dramatic, but it was hard to pump milk and have a nurse feed and hug him.

Being allowed and choosing are very different situations to be in. However, my family was the support system I needed at the time, and I am forever grateful to them for that. I was blessed to have my family around me during one of the most emotionally harrowing times of my life. While it was an emotional time for me then, I knew deep inside that situations like these happen in everyone's life, and I had to make peace with that.

## If Something Feels Wrong, Talk about it

We, women, in the deepest trenches of our souls, are sacrificial creatures. We tend not to share our pain and confusion with others very easily and instead focus on burying the negativity deep inside to fester over time. But here's the reality, your pain, whether emotional, physical, or mental, doesn't go away because you don't share it. The people around you cannot help you if you don't emote your feelings to them.

Women, as cliché as it sounds, also tend to overthink things. Especially when they are pregnant or have recently given birth because of the vulnerability and overwhelming hormonal changes they go through. When you overthink things, you will, for certain, end up having a negative mindset. When you are in such a vulnerable state, you must keep yourself motivated and tell yourself that you take each day as it comes. Your mantra needs to be 'one day at a time.'

It's silly to assume that your family cannot understand the emotions you are going through. Your family is your ultimate support system and will be there for you and your baby, no matter what. They're as emotionally vested in the situation as you are, and you can open up to them and trust in the fact that they won't let you down. If anything, you can always count on them to help keep negativity, in the form of gossipy neighbour aunties and distant family members, away from you in your time of need.

There is no shame in asking for professional help, especially if you begin to have depressive thoughts. Sometimes, no layperson or self-help book out there can help you, and you need someone well versed in that particular field to feel better. So, it is always good to seek expert help here. Even if you aren't dealing with depressive thoughts, visiting a specialist can help you navigate this new space in your life and adapt to the latest version of yourself.

## Glorifying Motherhood

Did you know that Mother's Day is the second most popular holiday in the US after the winter holidays? Other than the social media tributes thanking mothers for doing the impossible (being a mom is apparently akin to being a superhero on this particular day), I think we don't value our mothers enough.

Instead of normalising the struggles they have, we tend to put them on pedestals. While I am glad to know that we choose to honour mothers this way for all they do, I can't help but think that this glorification can put a lot of pressure on women to be 'the best mother in the world'. Motherhood is not a competition; it's all about raising a child in the best way you can.

Being the perfect mother is a nerve-wracking and impossible pursuit, and more people need to shout out from the rooftops about how motherhood is about flawed perfection. But, as I have said before, no mother is without her flaws. When you try to make your child your only priority, you give yourself reasons to build resentment from within.

Many of my friends are homemakers by choice, but they had thriving careers before they had their children. While a lot of them genuinely love the fact that they get to spend time seeing their children grow up, some tend to feel left out, or more accurately, left behind seeing the lives of others around them. Whatever a mother decides to do with her life is her choice. But when society glorifies certain life choices over others, it can create insecurities where they shouldn't be.

I think when we talk about glorifying mothers, it's also necessary to mention how easily society shames them. When you give birth to your child, you are given a tailor-made set of responsibilities that are in place for life. Therefore, how you choose to parent your child depends entirely on you and your partner.

For example, my husband and I have always been open about drinking alcohol in front of our son. I can practically hear close-minded people clutching at their pearls and gasping about this, but I couldn't be less bothered. There was an instance when my son, at two years old, was curious about the can of beer my husband was drinking from. So, my husband gave him a sip to assuage that curiosity. As soon as he tasted it, he screwed up his face and said it was 'very yucky'. He always steers clear of mom and dad's drinks now. Call it what you want, but that was a teachable moment for my son. That's the fun of parenting; there's no right way to go about it. So, if something seems like a good parenting strategy to you, do that.

Putting a moral value on a mother's choices doesn't empower her, instead, it cripples her self-development. If you want to glorify mothers, glorify ALL mothers. But let's all agree to stop shaming mothers for the choices they make, okay?

## I am not My Mother

I read somewhere that 'All women grow up and turn into their mothers'. God forbid that ever happens.

While it might have been a childhood dream to be like my own mother someday, I think as an adult, I am glad that I have become my own person, i.e., an untraditional kind of mom. Actually, in today's day and age, my unconventional approach to conducting myself as a mom might even be borderline normal. For my mother, unfortunately, my approach to motherhood is radical, to say the least.

The fact that I wanted to continue working after having a baby while not giving up the opportunities to grow further was quite confusing to my mother. She thought taking care of Aryan was a 24*7 job, and anything else would just detract from it. But, on the other hand, I knew that I didn't want to be the kind of mom who felt regret or blamed her child for missing out on things life had to offer.

I wish I could say motherhood made me a better daughter, but realistically, it gave me absolute clarity on how to live my life on my terms. My mom has a very different perception of motherhood from mine. While our thoughts might clash on the merits of homemade snacks over store-bought ones, she continues to be one of my biggest cheerleaders.

It goes without saying that growing up, I put my mother on a pedestal as well. Every child does because their mothers are the centre of their entire universe, making them the most important person to them. My mother, bless her, is one of the main reasons I am the woman I am today.

## Take Time to Love Yourself

I think a happy mom is the best mom. So, it is essential to make yourself happy before you can make your child or spouse happy. The easiest way to do this is by putting effort into your appearance and lifestyle. If you're working from home, make sure you're dressed up, even on non-meeting days. Try working from your desk, not the bed. Trust me; a little effort goes a long way.

Looking good and getting dressed can change your entire mindset. Vidhi Beri, a close friend, has been a constant source of inspiration here. She's always dressed to the nines, even at 8 in the morning, before breakfast is served! The way you're dressed and look can alter your mood. So, make getting dressed and feeling good a part of your daily routine. No matter what insecurities you may have, you feel assured when appreciated. When you take time and put the effort into yourself, it shows and speaks volumes.

# 7

# Moms Vs Compromise

*"In the end, I'm the only one who can give my*
*children a happy mother who loves life."*

**– Janene Wolsey Baadsgaard –**

If I forgo washing my hair and skip the pre toothbrushing karaoke, I can probably drop off Aryan to school, pick up some drive-through breakfast, and still get to work on time.

The precarious balancing act of motherhood depends greatly on a mom's ability to compromise and optimise their time. The power to do so doesn't come in one day but rather in phases. For the first year or so, a mother's entire routine depends on her child's sleep pattern. Since babies don't sleep in fixed intervals, it changes as time goes on. I was perhaps luckier than most in this aspect because my son was not the sort of baby to fuss over nap time. He would end up falling asleep whenever I would. That habit is so ingrained in him that even now, he naps with me on flights whenever we travel.

As your child grows older, their routine (and yours by proxy) stabilises to a sort of steady chaos. Sometimes, I think my husband has it a bit harder than I do. My son and I are the early birds in the house, while my husband remains a late riser. The poor man has had plenty of mornings where Aryan penalises him before he can even get out of bed. "Daddy bad, mommy good." This usually gets Aryan an hour of extra negotiated playtime with his dad and me some giggles, so all is well.

The reason I bring up my ever-changing morning routine is that post-motherhood, even something as mundane as your morning routine, can change, and the slightest compromise can affect your day (for better or for worse). Being a mom involves some serious mathematical ingenuity on an everyday basis, and unfortunately, compromises are part and parcel of that.

## Working Moms and Balance

For a brief period of time, I considered naming this book 'Baby Shark or Bureaucracy'. While I thankfully didn't, the name did encompass the moral struggle women have with maintaining careers or raising their children. Motherhood is essentially the art of precariously maintaining a fine balance. Choosing to have a career seems like a trade-off most mothers make after giving birth. However, it's never a 'this or that' situation. What one calls a trade-off, I call balance. No woman can be working and never taking care of her child and vice versa.

I genuinely think that there is absolutely nothing a mother cannot do when it comes to multitasking. Perhaps, some can say that we are biologically hardwired to be expert jugglers from birth. How well you balance your life depends on how good you are at multitasking and managing all the different facets of your life. But, of course, these trade-offs and balances keep on changing as time goes on.

Take me, for example. After my son started attending daycare around the age of 2, I made it a rule not to take on client meetings or work after 5 p.m. Instead, I would leave the office at 5, pick him up from daycare and spend the rest of the day with him exclusively. That was a decision I chose to make as a mom. You may consider it irrelevant, but it was a decision that affected how I approach work and is just another example of the many adjustments women need to continually make as their children grow older.

What made it easier for me to maintain a balance was studying my son's routine as he grew up. If you know how to regulate your child's core habits and sleeping patterns, you can adjust your own routine accordingly. Of course, it goes without saying that there probably won't be any burning of the midnight oil for a while, but at least you can strike a balance that keeps you happy (and sane).

## Avoid the 'Blame Game'

Let's be very honest. I agree that being a mom is a full-time job, but saying that motherhood is why you aren't pursuing your dreams is an excuse and a really bad one at that. Don't use your child as an excuse for your dreams not becoming a reality. Everyone has different circumstances, and I am aware this seems like a blanketed statement, but if you truly have something that is important to you, you will find a way to achieve it.

I wanted to talk about stay-at-home moms here too. When women decide to take care of their children and homes full time, it's a conscious decision on their part. For them, being front and centre of their child's growth and development is important. While I respect women who choose that, there can be times when they can start to regret their decision and feel overwhelmed by it.

I have my apprehensions about women who give up on their own ambitions and think that bringing up their children is their only purpose left. With the amount of technology and know-how available online, there's no excuse or end to what you can do, learn, and achieve in this world. Being a mother is not a hobby or a personality trait. To truly find fulfilment, I urge mothers to, at the very least, find diverse hobbies that diversify their skills, if not having a career of their own.

That being said, the pressure that comes with being a mom is incredibly overwhelming. To overcome those struggles, a mental balance is required to keep everything in check. When we talk about balance, we tend to focus on just the time management or physical space aspect of things, excusing mental wellness as 'self-care' that can be easily managed by using essential oils and scented candles. Unfortunately, that is not the case at all.

Laying down boundaries is an integral part of a mother's mental health. For example, I knew I needed to work a 9-5 job with set working hours in order to be there for my son. Spending quality time with Aryan was worth rescheduling meetings with important clients because that bonding time was something I was unwilling to compromise on. It's always easier to set apart when you understand that certain things are important and never worth conceding, no matter what.

## Taking Charge of Opportunities

We love a good girl boss moment, and it pleases me to no end to see that there's been a recent spike in mothers who have gone the entrepreneurship route these past few years. There is something so inspiring about women wanting to reclaim their careers and take charge of their situations.

As times have changed, so have the opportunities presented to mothers. I myself started a new business when I was pregnant. However, it didn't succeed overnight and was a product of taking small but sure steps since my son was born. Then, he was my top priority, but now that he's six years old, I know he can keep busy by himself and don't feel as guilty prioritising my work. My advice: Stop taking a perpetual break and get out of your comfort zone.

Nowadays, anything and everything can be monetised and, by proxy, be a legitimate career. Any passion or hobby can be utilised in a way that makes you money and allows you to thrive. For example, I have a friend who worked as a fashion designer, but after giving birth, she decided to be a stay at home mom. Instead of giving up on her passion, she started an Instagram page and posted sketches of her work. Through this page, she got many followers and offers of collaborations from businesses who were impressed by her designs. While she chose to not monetise on those opportunities, she still managed to do what she loved and capitalise on that happiness.

Society, traditionally, has only ever given women the opportunity to thrive at home as a homemaker or in their careers. One can never seem to have both, and maximising on both spaces is a no go. That's the narrative we've been sold so far. There is no manual that allows women to manoeuvre this bias on their own.

A woman's balanced life depends entirely on her personal circumstances and how she deals with constant compromises and adjustments to keep it steady. So, as long as you are doing what feels right for you, follow that path, and ignore the worries, judgements, and opinions others (very unhelpfully) show to keep you from achieving your dreams.

## Negotiables and Non-negotiables

We all have our lists of negotiables and non-negotiables in life. Watching Cocomelon in the evening?

Non-negotiable. McDonald's for dinner? Negotiable. If something is extremely important to you, it becomes non-negotiable, and you need to put your foot down and see it through. If you don't have the willpower to see it through, honestly (and pardon my French), stop whining about it.

I highly recommend all mothers jot down a list of what their personal negotiables and non-negotiables are. For example, I try to spend at least one hour of quality time with Aryan every single day, without fail. Sure, the lockdown has changed the entire dynamic, but when he was going to day-care, I made sure I went to pick him up every day to spend time with him, asking him how his day was, what he ate, if he had any problems, etc. Even asking him about unimportant things like the games he played or what cartoons he wanted to watch ensured that we stayed close despite my work.

Having a career of my own was also non-negotiable for me. Of course, it had been a slow and steady comeback post-birth, but I made sure I gave time to my work, despite my son being my foremost priority. Then, I had not wanted to leave my son at the mercy of daycare because I knew he would not be able to communicate with me and others till he was at least two years old. Now, I know my son has a high enough emotional intelligence to share with me.

Thinking through their own negotiables and non-negotiables can allow moms to lessen their anxiety by setting guidelines that help them deal with whatever life throws at them. It turns out that when you clearly define boundaries, you actually learn to manage your time and energy better.

## Is Compromise Damaging?

The word 'compromise' has highly negative connotations attached to it. This is because compromise means giving things up, to concede. But can compromising be healthy for mothers in the long run? I think so. Compromise is healthy if done right.

You might not like to hear it, but the fact remains that a woman's life is meant to take on certain compromises throughout its course. Some can call it adjusting or accommodating to situations, but let's call a spade a spade; it's just us compromising at the end of the day.

If there are changes in family life, the pressure of that change falls on the women of the family first. For example, while lockdown was tough on everyone, it was especially tough on women who weren't used to having husbands sitting on their heads all day long. Both my mother and mother-in-law have told me (in confidence) that they cannot wait for their husbands to get out of the house and leave them be!

All healthy relationships require some element of compromise to make them work. As long as one's non-negotiables are not conceded, meeting people halfway will help improve their quality of life and the way they communicate.

## Don't be Afraid of Setting Limits

When it comes to dealing with interfering family members and colleagues, the best course of action is to pick your battles. If they persistently make you uncomfortable, it is okay to put your foot down and distance yourself from those parties. It's not always necessary to be vocal about every issue you face; sometimes, you need to let your actions do the talking instead.

# 8

# Moms Vs Adjustment

*"She stood in the storm and when the wind didn't blow her way, she adjusted her sails."*

**– Elizabeth Edwards –**

As we faced a global pandemic, something radical happened. Mothers, the world around, seemingly evolved into a new species of superwomen overnight. Before they knew it, women suddenly had the ability to juggle full-time jobs alongside being a teacher, homemaker, and caregiver!

The Covid-19 pandemic left the world reeling, but despite this, two years later, we have all adapted to the new normal of social distancing, mandatory masks, and hand sanitisers reasonably well. It's because, inherently, human beings are adaptable creatures and can adjust to new situations quickly.

Even so, when I first heard about the initial lockdown, I had greatly underestimated the threat of Covid-19. But after three months of lockdown, I knew it was a situation we could no longer take lightly. That adjustment was a difficult transition for our son and us.

The crux of the matter was that while everyone had their own lifestyle, the disruption of routine created a mess like no other, and the newness of it all left all of us, especially women, scrambling for balance and sanity. While husbands and partners tried their best to help, the onus of childrearing and housework fell mainly on the mothers themselves, leading them to figure out the tumultuous times ahead with nothing to guide them.

## Mothers and the Covid-19 Crisis

While lockdown was tough on everyone, it was especially tough on women who weren't used to having husbands sitting on their heads at home all day long. I think it's become a cliché to say that lockdown brought everyone closer together. It might have been for the first month or so, but after that, everyone just wanted their everyday life back.

That being said, the post-Covid-19 era has altered the modern mom's life entirely. Recently, a woman came by my office to pick up her husband, who is my client. My husband, the client, and I were there, having a few beers, and since she came, I offered her one as well. After a can, she just broke down crying.

She started talking about how Covid made her life a living hell, how her kids were always at home, and that she didn't have anything for herself anymore. This lady, a big name in the exhibition industry, was suddenly without work and a steady income after the pandemic hit.

It must have been overwhelming, to say the least, and she desperately needed to vent and air out the pain she was feeling. I am happy she confided in us, and empathy is all I had for the poor woman.

When your life changes drastically due to circumstances totally out of your control, it's easy to feel overwhelmed by everything. For example, I had no domestic help this past year, and I was taking care of the cooking, husband, son, and everything else in the house by myself. That change in lifestyle was difficult to get used to because I didn't choose this forced change, and it altered my quality of life. I think just having more empathy and sympathy for women going through a tough time is an excellent way to support them. This could be shown through actions like spouses sharing more responsibilities, kids being less dependent, etc.

## Navigating the WFH Space

At the beginning of the pandemic, my morning routine used to be me literally rolling out of bed, sitting in front of the computer, and logging into work. Maybe with a cup of coffee in hand. It was after a conversation with my health coach, Vidhi Beri, that I realised all the negative energy I was harbouring during this time.

Her solution? Just get up, get dressed, and face the day like you would every other day pre covid. It didn't matter if people saw me or not, but to feel better and become more positive mentally, I needed to put some effort into my appearance. So, I did follow her advice and noticed a marked improved difference in my productivity and energy throughout the day. Later, my husband and I also took the initiative to set up a proper home office that allowed us to co-work from home in peace.

Co-working wasn't difficult for us at all, especially since our work is often done in tandem. In addition, ten years of marriage have taught us to understand each other's non-verbal cues, and it didn't take a lot of effort for us to navigate any issues that came up. Initially, as new parents, we did have trouble disconnecting our work lives from our personal lives, but after Aryan was born, we took the conscious decision to change our working arrangement so that we could make time for each other without work taking over.

Aryan, luckily for us, has also been so good at understanding and respecting that if Rahul (my husband) and I are working from home, he is not to disturb us unless something essential comes up. Kids are, in a way, more adaptive than adults. We still crave our safe spaces, but kids are curious and quickly adapt to whatever situations they see.

## Children and the Pandemic

These past two years have been so strange not only for the parents but also for the kids. In India, kids have not gone to school at all in the past two years. Here, in Kuala Lumpur, things have been relatively easier, and school resumed like always, albeit on an off and on basis. But, if you ask me as a parent, I think the most challenging part of the pandemic has been the transition to online learning.

Online school feels like more of a schooling experience for me rather than my son because, as a mom, I have to attend classes with him, making sure he understands and stays focused. I will readily admit that I get anxious and a little cranky when teaching him. So, when I get angry, he starts drawing a heart on his textbook and then breaking it apart while saying, "This is Aryan's heart, and mummy has broken the love." I think his drama skills come genetically from me.

Though it's a very useful tactic, he's picked up and almost immediately gets me out of my bad mood. As a mom, it's challenging to teach your child because your child thinks of you in a very different role. I try to make sure he thinks of learning as fun because, honestly, I don't care about his marks in trigonometry or algebra as long as he grows up street smart.

Lockdown has also made him navigate the home space better. While he respects our space when it comes to work, we also take the time out to understand his feelings and help him figure out whatever is bothering him. I get that a certain amount of impatience starts to trickle in when you spend all day with children, but these times are confusing for them too. They need help and understanding from their parents to guide them through the uncertainties they experience.

## Things ALL Working Mothers should Know

As an entrepreneur, I agree that there are definitely certain benefits I experience that moms who are salaried employees do not. While I have the liberty to take my own days off and take my son to work whenever I need to, it is not all fun and games. Being an entrepreneur mom has its own set of advantages and disadvantages because I have a lot of other responsibilities I need to take charge of, all at the same time.

The point I'm making here is that even if I have certain freedoms, I still face the same struggles as any other working mom. Overall, however, the most significant advantage of being in the entrepreneurial space is balancing and managing my time much better.

I believe that all working moms, and even stay-at-home moms, can easily be overwhelmed, especially if they have not prioritised a routine for themselves. However, if they had a proper routine and decent time management skills, they would find that the balancing act is not as tricky as it seems.

The biggest struggle unbalanced moms seem to have is that their lack of routine causes them to spend too much time at work and not enough at home, or vice versa. You will be surprised to know that in the grand scheme of things, it is not important to spend too much time in your career or even too little, as long as you make sure your happiness comes first.

If your work makes you happier than taking care of your child, stop feeling guilty and look for the right kind of childcare system that will support you. Remember, if you can't be a happy person, you cannot be a good mom. Your happiness needs to come first, especially if you want to keep your child and family happy. If you don't, your actions will show how miserable you feel. So do not be afraid to take action, and if it calls for certain adjustments, please do it without any guilt.

## The Working Parent Guilt

The idea of making parents feel guilty for working too much is an outdated concept, to say the least. We live in the twenty-first century now, so everyone who thinks that working parents are absent parents should go back to the fourteenth century, where that ideology belongs.

Kids who grow up in a household with two working parents don't grow up undisciplined and constantly seeking attention. On the contrary, a well-rounded and grounded upbringing results from a loving home, nothing more and nothing less.

Workplaces are now opening up creches and daycares to help support employees in dire need of childcare, it is still quite a novel concept for the most part.

I never had domestic help to take care of Aryan, preferring the professionally monitored and safe space day-cares provided instead. Even so, I took care of him full-time till he was two years old, but now, if asked, I genuinely think going to day-care now has made him a more social, outgoing, and independent child.

For mothers facing down this 'parental guilt', my advice is this: treasure your happiness and don't give in to the outdated thoughts of the naysayers around you. Do what makes you happy instead. Don't give in to peer pressure or the comparison guilt. As women, we need to play a lot of roles in life. Just because your journey is different from those around you doesn't make it wrong. So, focus on your unique path, and be unapologetic about the decisions you make. You've got this!

## Make Time to bond with Your Kids

During the pandemic, the lines between working and being at home were blurred, and I needed to make sure I spent adequate time bonding with my son instead of just being there for him. I think this holds true for all parents. Ask yourself this: When was the last time you did activities with your child and not just spent time with them in front of a television screen?

Some of the fun activities you can do together include watching movies together, playing with kinetic sand, etc. Try painting with your kids – it doesn't even have to be very detailed, just paint your hands and stick them on a piece of paper, or use delivery boxes for arts and crafts, swimming, cycling, etc. Don't be afraid to get messy; kids love activities that create sensory stimulation.

# 9

# Moms Vs Social Media

*"Social media is meant to connect you to like-minded people. Don't let it twist your idea of perfect because of those pretending to be "mom of the year" out there."*

**– Shikha Kedia Bharadwaj –**

The insanity of social media can be overwhelming. Just think back to two years ago, when Covid-19 hit the world? Then, people actually blamed Corona – the beer – for spreading Coronavirus. Sales dropped drastically initially, then overwhelmingly shot through the roof when people realised they were being silly and missing out on good beer.

In another beer-related incident, I posted a picture of my son on Instagram a few years back. Immediately I got a DM from a 'concerned' older acquaintance of mine. Why? Because my son, three years old at the time, was wearing a t-shirt with the Heineken logo on it. This acquaintance thought it was inappropriate for my son to wear the t-shirt (which he looked adorable in FYI) because it 'glorified alcohol.' Needless to say, both the message and acquaintance were ignored after that.

Social media, for me, is a happy space, so I usually prefer to ignore the nonsense I hear in favour of the good stuff. However, the kind of influence social media has on a person depends on how you, the user, use it. For example, my father-in-law watches and follows many news networks talking about how bad the current government is. So much so that the only conversation at the dinner table, regardless of it being in Kolkata or Kuala Lumpur, is about how inept they are. He does it so often that my mother-in-law has put out an official statement saying that if politics is brought up at the table at any given time, no dinner gets served!

Most people would rather think that Google is listening and recording their conversations than believe that social media sites and apps constantly bombard them with targeted news and advertisements based on their profiles and search histories. So, if you are anti-government, you will see that kind of content and vice-versa.

Because my father-in-law may have been profiled in a certain way, he only saw harmful content, negatively impacting him. We need to be cognizant of using social media as intellectuals, and with the influx of so much information online, it's important to verify everything sent to us by making sure the sources are legitimate and only then form an opinion. Social media as a resource is fantastic if used right if you don't believe everything you see on the internet.

## The Modern Mom and Social Media

With respect to modern-day mothers, social media's impact has been immense and has helped destigmatise a lot of things. In addition, the willingness of mothers, influencers, and celebrities to share their authentic thoughts and opinions regarding issues like postpartum depression and other struggles has been transformative.

Of course, these issues have always been there, but the act of sharing their struggles online suddenly made it okay for other mothers to publicly discuss them without shame. At a time when women second-guessed and hid their feelings about these so-called 'taboo' topics, speaking up about it changed lives.

The internet has now become an incredibly important source of information. From breastfeeding support groups on Facebook to helpful Reddit forums, one can discuss their feelings, anxieties, and so much more on a global level. Social media has become an information exchange medium and helps mothers stay updated on relevant topics, which is very important for all modern moms.

## Keyboard Warriors: The bad side of Social Media

Ah, the negative, judgemental side of social media. We've all had experiences with it. Most of the time, I choose to ignore the trolls and keyboard warriors, but there are times when their opinions get to me. Recently, I was invited for lunch after a particularly hard day at work by friends, who insisted on catching up. By now, you all know that I try to balance my personal and work life whenever I can, so I ended up going and having the most therapeutic and healing time with them.

After getting back home, I put up a story with the caption, "In between everyday hustle, always find time for lunch with my girls #Happybalancedlife." Somehow, this innocent story made some of my acquaintances and followers feel the need to reply, "girls???" on it, even as many others gave love to the picture. Despite not wanting to engage with that negativity, I felt like I had to say something, so I did in the politest way I could, 'Thank you for your opinion, but I don't need your judgement.'

While I wasn't hurt by what they implied, this incident did make me realise the judgement we, as women, go through every day. People on the internet rarely feel the consequences of their actions immediately, so they like to post comments and opinions with loose lips. It's no secret that social media is full of judgement. This negativity makes trying to see the positive side of things more complicated, allowing us to get side-tracked by the negative side, i.e., trolling, commenting, and cyberbullying.

But sometimes, unsolicited opinions are not all bad, at least if taken in the right way. For example, when Aryan was a newborn, I posted a picture of him and me together, and someone commented that I should not be holding him the way I was. While I thought the way I was holding him was perfectly fine, I tried to take their opinion positively. Maybe they were just being thoughtful in their own way.

Mothers face judgement for everything they do on social media, so much so that it's almost become a fact of life at this point. Everything from not having bounced back to their pre-baby bodies fast enough to posting too many pictures of their kids online, even feeding them cookies over apples for snacks, has become a contentious issue on the Internet.

Unfortunately, the judgement never stops. People will continue to put every single aspect of your life under a microscope. My advice for dealing with these sorts of people is to use the 'mute' and 'block' buttons liberally, and if they offer suggestions, either acknowledge them or ignore them. Just don't waste time trying to appease them because that is futile.

## 'Picture Perfect' isn't Real Life

Everything has a good and bad side, and social media is no different. There is a glaring need for people to be more authentic on the Internet because the pursuit of perfection creates a toxic cycle for others. Social media's penchant for filtering things has definitely impacted mothers as well. For example, I follow a lot of moms on Instagram, and I love when they share pictures of their postpartum bodies with their stretch marks on display to let people know that this is the body they should be expecting.

If you aren't comfortable sharing authentic photographs on social media, then feel free not to. But please don't paint a falsely filtered picture-perfect image that is simply not real. I'm not saying that you need to stop putting up selfies with cute filters, but it's a different topic altogether when discussing serious subjects like one's motherhood journey.

Don't paint a falsely rosy picture of your life and struggles. If you've worked really hard to get the body of your dreams, own the effort it took to get you there and share your journey. When people see how much time, energy, and motivation it took to get there, they will support you and, moreover, get inspired by your hard work and authentic approach to your goals.

Living a picture-perfect existence isn't reflective of a happy life. So, instead of using social media as a crutch to feel bad about yourself, try to fill your network with people who inspire and motivate you.

## Maintaining a Healthy, Balanced Relationship with Social Media

Most people find it very funny when I tell them I am terrible at managing my own social media handles because I am so busy doing it for others. However, I actually prefer it that way because it allows me to use social media as a tool to destress rather than be a stressor itself. Social networking can become overwhelming, and to maintain a balanced relationship with social media, it is important for one to always follow their instincts and not take social media too seriously. Because I come from a digital marketing background, I have a reasonably good idea of whether what I see online is fake or not. While this insight comes naturally to me, it might not be the same for others.

To maintain a healthy relationship with social media, change the way you approach it. These social networking platforms are a valuable resource to learn and exchange ideas. For example, Facebook has so many mom groups where you can connect with peers from every corner of the world and get queries answered instantly. Even professional networking sites like LinkedIn have become a safe space for mothers in business, and people are incredibly positive to comment, help and support women's career pathways.

Everyone displays a perfect version of themselves on social media. Because of that impossible standard, I urge people to take everything with a pinch of salt and not set unrealistic goals for themselves. Life is much more profound and exciting than what you see online. Don't compare your journey with others and criticise yourself for not being able to achieve a certain kind of ideal.

I see this happen a lot in parents. People keep comparing their kid's achievements to that of another's when they should be supporting their children going and growing on their own journey. When you follow someone, understand they have been through certain things to be where they are in life. You haven't gone through that, so do not compare your journey with theirs.

## Social Media and Self Image

In a world where we equate the likes on a selfie with validation, it's tough not to let social media play a crucial role in how we perceive ourselves. Unfortunately, most people forget that they had a life before social media came into existence, and they'll continue to have one after. Social media hype cannot define you or your self-worth. It's as simple as that.

Even though I come from a digital marketing background, I personally think it is healthy for people not to display their entire lives on the internet and keep some moments private. For example, just because you didn't post pictures of your last date night doesn't mean your love life isn't going well. It just means you didn't want to share a private moment with the world at large. Similarly, if one chooses to keep their life confidential, you must respect that and not judge them for it. Many millennials nowadays are reclaiming their privacy on social media because of their burnout from using it.

The assumption that a person's presence online is reflective of their mental and emotional well-being is ridiculous. There is life beyond social media. We've all met at least one person who has asked us an inappropriate (and silly) question like, "I haven't seen you post something in a while. Is everything okay?" According to the world, we are what we display on our Instagram grid. If we aren't sharing our life online, we aren't truly enjoying it.

It has become so commonplace to share photos of what you have eaten, what flights you are taking, the vacation you are on, etc., that we don't even think about why we engage in it. The short answer? Validation. If you post pictures of what you ate and where you went on holiday to maximise the experience, go ahead. Embrace your passion! But, if you think that it is the defining factor or very reason for doing it, you are letting it affect your self-worth. Instead, I urge my readers to live in the present and disconnect whenever overwhelmed. Put your happiness, mental, and physical health first, always.

## Take Everything You see on Social Media with a Pinch of Salt

Every time you see someone putting up a perfectly posed picture on social media, calling it candid, remember this: they are lying. It's only a candid picture if someone is mid-blink, with their double chin showing. You can't convince me otherwise. Similarly, that perfect picture you saw of a celebrity? It was the result of hours of planning. Instead, I urge you to be authentic. People trust realness and appreciate authenticity. If you have pictures of you doing things with perfect hair and outfits, we know you took more effort for the picture than you did for the activity itself.

There's also an overload of unverified information on the internet. For example, let's take the online fear campaign against getting vaccinated for Covid-19. Everyone seems to have become a doctor regarding the effectiveness of the vaccine. Instead of spreading unverified and potentially dangerous information, do your due diligence and then make an informed decision.

# 10

# Moms Vs Balance

*"For me, success is not a destination,*
*it's a journey of a happy, balanced life."*
**– Shikha Kedia Bharadwaj –**

We have such a skewed understanding of what living a balanced life entails. It's not about balancing a school bag in one hand and a briefcase in another; it's about transforming the way you approach your life. Moms need to cultivate the practice of balance and not live in chaos because, let's face it, a lot of household responsibilities fall into their lap, and instead of drowning in them, they deserve to thrive.

Everything from our body to our life has to have a good balance in order to work well. The whole reason I wanted to write this book in the first place was to help women gain this balance. Time and time again, I have seen so many women excel at their careers and burn out because they could not strike a balance between their personal and professional lives. There are three core components of a woman's life, i.e., her career, her family, and herself. Maintaining a balance between these three spaces is especially important for a woman because she will not have a happy life or be mentally and physically structured unless she has this balance.

Having a good balance among various aspects of your life does affect the quality of your life. Your lack of routine, in the simplest of terms, means that you are not planning the rest of your life properly. Taking it in as it comes is good when it comes to unforeseen circumstances but will affect your personal and family life in the long run. When you have a routine, not an extremely strict one, mind you, you know when it's time for family, work, or yourself.

Staying in Kuala Lumpur, away from my homeland, has changed the way I look at mothers. Mothers are powerful, strong women. As I have said before, I am deeply inspired by the women here because while they have minimal maternity leave, they have the best work-home life balance I have seen. The women here know how to balance and work hard to maintain it. Meanwhile, in India, we encourage women to hide away during most of their pregnancies because families believe it's better to handle things discreetly. Times, access to information, and the Internet have since made us realise that being pregnant is not something we should have to hide. Your pregnancy and motherhood journey shouldn't feel like the end of your life.

## Family and Balance

It's a very Asian thing to expect women to keep families together. For women, family always comes first. But living in a family-centric environment can have its own issues when there is a breakdown in communication and responsibilities. Communication is a major part of family life.

In a family-centric environment, everyone has certain responsibilities towards each other. Until you know your responsibilities, you will not be able to strike a balance and have a happy relationship with the other people in the house. That is why it is important to have a good routine. Make it a point to talk and reflect with your family at least once a day. There is a sense of breakage in that balance if you don't.

Those small efforts you make in your life to set up a small routine, and if you do not do something like calling them, you break that balance and make them unhappy, and ultimately, yourself as well, because your actions have repercussions. So, to combat this, set smaller routines, whatever is feasible for you, know your responsibilities and incorporate them into your routine.

## Children and Balance

I've always been a firm believer in the fact that the greatest lesson you could ever teach your children comes from how you conduct your life and not what you preach to them. For example, my son has a deep sense of balance. He wakes up at 7 am sharp, knows by 7.30 that he will have breakfast, and has a proper routine that comes naturally to him for the rest of the day. I don't want to toot my horn by saying that he gets that from me or if it's just something inherent in him, but unconscious learning comes naturally to kids.

Even when I am sleeping, my son knows not to wake me up. My mother-in-law once told me that when I had crashed unusually early one night after a long flight, my son was going around telling everyone in the house not to make noise because his mom was sleeping. Likewise, if I'm on a call, he won't let anyone make noise. He makes that effort because he understands my way of life and structure. That's why I say how you conduct your life is how your kids will lead their lives.

Children are the ones that get impacted the most by their parents' erratic unbalanced schedules. Guiding them is not just what you are teaching them but also how you lead your own life. What you do has the biggest impact on your kids. The way you perceive yourself is how your children perceive you. So, start taking yourself and your actions seriously, and give yourself as much love and importance as you want your child to have for themselves.

## Flexibility and Balance

While planning and routine are paramount to balance, I do agree that life has to be flexible, especially for a new mom or a mother with a growing child. I'm all for living wild and free, but I recommend having a baseline routine in place, regardless. For example, there have been times when I cannot commit to meetings at the last minute because of unforeseen circumstances, but most people can work around them if you're honest about what you are going through.

Having a routine is very important, but it does need to be flexible to work. There might be days you cannot work because of other commitments, or when your family life requires more time than your career, it is on those stressful days the whole balancing act comes in, especially if you have a flexible routine in place. On the other hand, if you don't have a routine, trying to tackle a balanced lifestyle is of absolutely no use to you because you aren't trying hard enough to build one.

Just yesterday, I met a friend after four long years, and we ended up catching up on each other's lives. We had gotten married around the same time, but she had her child a lot earlier than I did. When her kid was 7 years old, she decided she wanted to study law, which was a big step, especially for a stay-at-home mom. I was very proud of her for taking that step then. After graduating in law four years later, she wanted to set up her own law firm with the help of her husband. Her husband was hesitant to help her out, knowing that work would be an added responsibility that she might not be able to handle, on top of being a mother to a 10-year-old. She, however, was determined to make her dream come true and not give up when she was so close to achieving it. I continue to admire her for that tenacity.

Mothers who have a vision, focus, and a routine in place find it easier to remain balanced versus moms who are more impulsive, which is an indisputable fact. When you are planning ahead, you are utilising time well. A planned life increases your productivity and adds more value to your everyday wellbeing. When you start living your life like that, you will notice that you suddenly have more time to do the things you want, whereas before, you struggled to find time, even for yourself.

## Trusting The Balance

As I have mentioned before, marriage is an excellent teacher when it comes to teaching you to be a more patient person. Having a child is just an accelerating force guiding you towards that patience. That patience is what you need to accommodate balance into your life. Things might or might not fall into perspective right away, but you have got to trust the process and take whatever happens as it comes.

There might even be times when you go off routine for a while, but simply panicking and giving up will not help. You have to handle all problematic matters practically and deal with them calmly. I think Covid-19 has taught us that. We all had special plans for 2020, which simply didn't come true. It was the same for me. I'm the kind of person who plans two years ahead. When that sense of routine was broken, I felt uncomfortable but ultimately decided to make adjustments and changes according to the situation at hand.

Let me give you an example. In May of 2020, my husband and I had a plan to set up an office and expand our business in the UK. By March, we knew it wasn't going to happen, and now I know that the dream of setting up an office there has been postponed for five years, at the very least. We were actually lucky in a way because Covid-19 hit the world entirely by March; I hate to think of the troubles we would have faced if we were already in the middle of setting things up. Yet, that didn't stop our professional growth.

You have to keep an open mind and be flexible with your plans, as my husband and I did when we embraced the unexpected while adjusting to current affairs. My husband came up with a new virtual event software during that time, helping the business grow when others were folding. Usually, I travel two months a year, so I decided to put my passion on paper and write a book with the time I saved instead. I chose to not worry about what could have been and focused on my reality, making the most of my circumstances.

## The Definition of a Successful Woman

According to the internet, a successful woman is someone who has the virtue of Mother Teresa, the body of Tyra Banks, the brains of Indra Nooyi, and the jokes to rival Twinkle Khanna. Basically, an impossibly perfect woman. While I love and respect all the incredibly successful women I have mentioned here, I will never try to aspire to be like them because I am not them. My journey is my own.

Why? Because success on its own is a very subjective term. Ever heard of the adage, 'One man's trash is another man's treasure?' Success is like that. There is no milestone to success; it can be anything to everything for people. For example, someone could earn 700 dollars a month, for others, it could be millions of dollars. The measure of what it means to be successful is different for different people.

Given that success is so subjective, the ultimate indicator of a successful life (according to me) is living a happy and balanced life. I think a person who is happy, inside and out, is the most successful person out there. As long as you love the life you live and give the most to whatever you do, you are on the pathway to success.

The most fascinating thing about quantifying success like this is how achievable it is. Your quality of life, mental and emotional health, relationships, etc., benefit significantly from simple acts like having a routine, planning ahead and prioritising yourself.

So, are you ready to have a happy, balanced life from today?

## Have a Daily Balanced Routine

Everyone's version of a balanced life is tailored to their specifications. However, there are failsafe essentials that every woman must follow to help her get started. Here are a few!

- Take fifteen to thirty minutes with yourself in the morning to plan your day, freshen up your mind, and feel happy. If a cup of tea or coffee is important to the endeavour, go for it!

- You feel good when you look good. Getting ready is very important even if you are alone at home, so dress up nicely, and you will find an immediate difference in your confidence, productivity, mood, and outlook.

- Figure out a fixed daily work and family schedule to better organise your day. For example, try to set up a plan to have one daily meal with the whole family, fun activities with kids, or a weekly date night with your spouse.

- Practice self-love and embrace the chaotic whirlwind woman you are. Remember, unless you love yourself, don't expect people to love you. So, choose to be kind to yourself.

# Experts Speak

In this special section, inspiring women share candid takes on breaking taboos and redefining the definition of what being a modern-day woman is all about.

- A Mother's Dream

  *(Sayantani Sen)*

- The Breakthrough

  *(Anuranjita Garodia)*

- Dream Big, Grow Bigger

  *(Dr. Meghana Dikshit)*

- Ready, Set, Go – The Great Motherhood Race

  *(Fatima Khanom)*

- I Want To Be Like My Mum

  *(Coco Wong)*

# A Mother's Dream

*(A Mom who never gave up on her dreams)*

**– Sayantani Sen –**

*(Communications @ The India Story | Neotia Arts Trust)*

It is 4.15 am, and my alarm vibrates. It could only be a mother's imagination to have the alarm vibrate and not scream aloud to disturb the others out of slumber! There are so many things that you would possibly never have imagined doing yet do most spontaneously because you think and act as only a mother can.

It is like motherhood carves an entirely different person out of you – the tigress and the saint blended together almost seamlessly. What you gain is patience – oodles and oodles of utmost patience, and what you give up is sleep – hours and hours of peaceful sleep!

Yet, if I were to talk about this journey – I would call it the most rewarding for all the things that come with the territory. I am what I am because of my daughters. They inspire me, anger me, fulfil me, trigger me but, above all, they complete me. I am most resilient and most enduring when I think of them.

One of these tales of resilience and endurance has been the journey of writing my thesis. I enrolled in a doctoral programme when my elder daughter was just a few months old amid a whole lot of opinions about how thoughtless and illogical the step was. Honestly, I hadn't thought about the practicalities of the decision then. It appeared logical to me since I had completed my M.Phil. a couple of years ago, took an executive course at the London School of Economics and Political Science to position my subjective orientation towards research and felt I was academically ready for this at last. I didn't know what all was to be expected of motherhood. I was a mother only the first time and for only a few months. I always knew the career was simultaneous with motherhood, so there was no apparent conflict about the decision in my head.

The first few years of PhD in fact, were fairly smooth. I had an M.Phil., and according to UGC rules back then, I did not need to attend classes at the University. All that was required of scholars like me was to stay in regular contact with our supervisor during and following the official registration of the thesis. So, after the initial legwork with research questions and hypothesis, there was a slumber into which the business of mothering the girls had comfortably fallen. By now, I had another girl (they were only two and a half years apart), and I did not remember that I was a research scholar as well for most of the day. I was working but managed to sustain that with the girls, and their periodic doctor's visits and so on were clubbed in as well.

Before I knew it, five years had gone by. Only then did I realise that I had exhausted the legitimate five years awarded to us as PhD scholars to submit our thesis. And that's when the hourglass turned, and I had a ton of paperwork to file to get an official extension (which, again, is fairly common). Once that was done, there was no running away from the fact that I had to get cracking on actually penning down the thesis now.

The last five years have been barely intermittent with thesis work. To break away from the mundaneness of it, I had taken up work with a design festival in the city, and although it was light and fun, to begin with, it soon began taking more than a little of my headspace and physical energy. My days were packed, and nights were tired. I had no viable plan to squeeze in writing time. And it wasn't just leisure writing. It had to be fully proofed, footnoted, logically argued and researched writing of chapters.

Just when I was almost ready to give it all up, my supervisor sat me down and told me this was completely doable. She explained to me my assets, neglecting the chore of liabilities that surrounded the job and for that hour with her, I quite forgot about the hurdles that lay ahead as well. But forgetting about something doesn't make it disappear. For a moment, I can think like Scarlett O' Hara and pretend that "Tomorrow is another day…" but tomorrow does bring with it its fair share of problems.

I knew I had to figure the way and at least give it a shot before I gave up. My daughters are young, and they hopefully wouldn't remember or complain about how little involved I was with their studies and school when I was focusing on my own writing. Yet the guilt of it was wrenching quite often, especially at moments when I felt I was giving a lot more time to my studies than theirs. And each time, I told myself that I would have enough opportunities to make up for all this and more. I knew I was buying time mentally and just trying to push those thoughts away to keep the brain productive and swift.

Thus began my gruelling schedules. I slotted myself 2-hour windows of research and writing around the schedules of my girls and the family. I tried to fit these in when they would leave for school, before work and after work. Soon I realised that after work was not working too well. I used to be too exhausted to focus and would not be able to make much progress in the evenings.

These were also windows when there would be more breaks to meet the demands of more family and people and answer many more questions – most of them disturbingly mundane. They would leave me more frustrated and remotely focused, but I also decided to keep this journey all to myself through them. I had not told anyone that I was finally starting to write the thesis. By this time, friends and family had thought I had given up on the PhD. Too long a time had passed, and I must have lost interest, gotten busy with other things and lost the focus needed to finish an enterprise of that volume and stature.

So, the quiet study time had to be reworked into very early morning schedules when the rest of the house was asleep. I began to work from 3 in the morning up to about 6.30 and never quite eased into the relentlessness of my schedule. This continued for almost a year through the ups and downs of rewriting chapters, arranging footnotes, and compiling statistics, figures, charts and graphs until I was ready to print the manuscript. The relief when the file reached the printer was unmatched. It was such an enormous weight off my shoulder. But even then, no one else was party to the progress of the thesis. Some part of me perhaps still doubted that something might go wrong, so I waited to share it with others. Finally, I submitted the thesis, and it was another six months of waiting to defend it before experts and students until I could be cleared for the degree. I remained on tenterhooks even then. A large part of me possibly did not believe that I had actually come that far.

Putting the memory of those endless nights behind me, I was ready to finally receive the degree on the morning of 24th December 2019, cloaked in the saffron University robe, waiting for the photograph that held the power to inspire a lifetime of my journey. But the share of drama wasn't done yet. The Governor, the Chancellor of the University, wasn't allowed inside the gates by protesting students, and a whole bunch of us waited for 3 hours, not knowing if we would even receive the degrees we had waited this long to hold in our hands. In time, however, we received the degree on the same day, perhaps with a lesser glamour around us but no less sense of accomplishment.

I shared the news with family only once I had the invite to the graduation in hand. The reaction from everyone was unmistakable – complete disbelief, almost shock, for it felt no less than magic to them. How did this girl finish it – we never saw her study or write. When did she do it? But those answers did not matter anymore. I was a Doctor after seven long relentless years of intense labour, the loneliness of unproductivity, endless sleep deprivation, troublesome paperwork and the absolute thrill of completion. I felt numb over the success of the achievement. Perhaps it happens when you have waited this long for the fruition of an enterprise.

It is 2022 now, and I have barely used the 'Dr' before my name. But the pride my daughters feel every time they say it makes all this more than worthy of all the years of tireless effort. When I look back, my daughters latently inspired me to continue, irrespective of the end.

The early morning habit has stayed with me, though it isn't the unearthly 3 AM anymore. But I use the morning to sort myself for the day. It is my time to pray and meditate, feed the birds and talk to my plants, feel the wet grass under my feet and ground myself to the blessings of the Universe.

# The Breakthrough

## (A Mom who defied all odds)

**– Anuranjita Garodia –**

*(Artist, Interior Designer & Relationship Counsellor)*

They say there is a reason, 'I AM ANURANJITA!' They say that time will heal.... it's been more than twelve long years, but it hasn't changed the way I feel. I still ask myself WHY??? It is hard enough losing the person you love and had planned to grow old with, coping with the grief, pain, shock and disbelief, but so much harder when you have to help a young, impressionable child deal with his too.

My son was merely seven when life happened.... our perfect life was turned upside down...EVERY SINGLE THING CHANGED. We were handed a new life that we never asked for or wanted. In the words of Benjamin Allen, "I entered the After loss broken and shattered. It's like I had this big bag of fragments I once called life and dumped them in the middle of this new World and said, "Here. This is all I've got left. What can I do with this?"

Suddenly from being a couple to a single mom, being responsible for everything... Parenting, everyday life, routine days, social obligations, it was overwhelming. In the beginning, the grief is so raw, so pure that it is the most gut-wrenching, agonizing thing to live with... Along with that, we had to face social stigma from certain quarters, the looks, the questions, the rejections or worse, the pity.

But it does get better, in the sense, you learn to live with it; you learn to smile again; You learn to appreciate the beauty and joys around without the constant guilt.

Being a single parent means double the work, double the stress, and double the challenges. It requires a single parent to combine the roles of two people with raising the children and running around with life!

Along with looking after my son came the added responsibility of taking up a job and leaving my little one behind. The pressure, the heartache, and the self-doubt was sometimes overwhelming, but with God's Grace, I slowly overcame these and worked hard and sincerely toward not only fulfilling my son's desires but also my childhood dream of travelling. I visited EUROPE, the mesmerizing beautiful cities and countries like Scotland, London, Paris, Venice, Murano Burano, Austria, Switzerland, Germany, Belgium, Norway, Finland, Denmark, Tallin, Sweden etc and our very own Leh,Ladakh.

Meditation, spiritual meets, music and long drives to nowhere became my constant companions to keep away the loneliness and sleepless nights at bay. Close family and friends' support helped a lot. I can't imagine negotiating through this all without them, especially my sister Miku, my brother Ashwini, my brother-in-law Anurag, my sister-in-law Megha, my uncle Vijay, my aunt Meena, my friends Ajay Bhaiya, Ritu Bhabhi, Neelam and the Millenium Moms to name a few. Today, if you ask me, how was my journey so far? I would say, "I picked up those fragments and turned them into something beautiful, maybe a little flawed but beautiful."

When I look at my, now soon to be twenty, strapping young lad Pradyumn.... I realize all the struggles; all the challenges were worth it. May I be able to empower him with roots and wings and may those be strong enough to take him through life.

I don't live my life in regret. All my experiences have moulded me into the person I am today. I've taken my weaknesses and turned them into strengths. I am unstoppable.

*Kyunki Waqt Ka Kaam Hai Dhalna... Dhal Jayega...* This, too, shall pass.

## – Jai Shree Krishna –

*क्यों न थोड़ा अलग बने,*
*खुश रहने की सलाह न देकर,*
*खुश रहने की वजह बने।*

# Dream Big, Grow Bigger

*(A Mom who found strength through her child)*

**– Dr. Meghana Dikshit –**

*(Leading Brain & Performance Expert)*

I was 28 years old when I had Pratham. They say that becoming a mother is a life-altering experience, and I can say, having been a mother for 19 years, that is absolutely true. It has been a privilege to watch him grow up to be a fine young man and see my life transform for the better alongside him.

I came from a family where comparison was commonplace, with my father often comparing my siblings and me. While I consider myself to be a conscious person, there are times I slip up. There was this one time I wanted Pratham to do something, and instead of asking him directly, I said something like, 'your friend does this without being asked to. Why can't you?' He just looked at me and told me that he would do whatever I asked of him, as long as I didn't start comparing him to other people, as he didn't like that. That's when I realised that I needed to stop pushing him in a manner I myself hadn't appreciated when I was a child. It's moments like this where I understood that motherhood is an ever-evolving process, and I am lucky to have a child that holds me accountable and allows me to grow as a parent.

I wish I could say I have an ironclad 'fool-proof' philosophy regarding motherhood, but it's not that simple. More than anything, I learned how to be a mother alongside him. As I evolved and learned as a parent, I wanted him to embody and absorb that ability: to learn, grow, and challenge himself constantly. I like to believe that he is a self-assured young man today because he is continually reflecting on himself, his achievements, and learning from his failures.

Knowing and being able to read yourself is fundamental to understanding the world and yourself better. I think everyone can benefit from a little introspection. Ask yourself this: What is it that you need to do to be better than the person you currently are?

The journey hasn't been completely rose-tinted, however. Motherhood rarely is. If I had to pick one thing that changed for me post-motherhood, it would be that I was no longer as carefree as I was before. I had a child who depended on me, and I think that for years together, I stopped thinking of myself first, and I put him first. Even today, every action and behaviour I take is like a mother first, keeping in mind how it will impact my son in his psychology and his future.

In all truth, the illusion of balance that women (primarily mothers) seek does not exist. What only matters is how you can be in harmony with what YOUR word is every day. Regarding balancing work and kids, Nora Roberts says, "Balance is a juggling act. The key to juggling is to know that some of the balls you have in the air are made of plastic & some are made of glass."

She continued, "And if you drop a plastic ball, it bounces back, no harm done. If you drop a glass ball, it shatters, so you have to know which balls are glass and which are plastic and prioritise catching the glass ones. It is hard to drop any ball, but if they were plastic, they would still be okay tomorrow."

So, I maintained my sanity by keeping my eye on the big picture and still focusing on the tiny everyday things when necessary. Which ball is important when? Whether it's handling family, paying attention to my son, my work, my focus is on whatever situation requires it most at that moment.

I owe all my success today, be it in my relationships, health, career, or everything I have done, entirely to my son. When he was born, the one thing I realised was that I could either continue to live a life of mediocrity like I did back then or take charge of the opportunity God gave me to raise my son, make him break barriers, and reach high standards. That meant that if I wanted to set high standards for my child, I had to set high standards for myself. I wanted him to find the role models he needed right here, at home. That is why I say that Pratham made me who I am today because he not only made me a better parent but a better version of myself, someone I am proud to present in this world.

His development has not been a solo effort. I would also like to credit his coaches, whom he's had since he was 7 years old, for making him the person he is today. When I started the journey of reinventing myself, I took him along to every self-development and personal development workshop I attended. That exposure and access to so many amazing coaches and mentors worldwide gave him a different perspective on life and helped make his thinking very independent. In a way, his experiential learning translated and dictated the trajectory of his physical life.

Since becoming a mother, I have had the privilege of being a better version of myself and contributing and adding value to the lives of others. The whole journey came from a lot of love because of the bond I had with my son. It made me whole in my demeanour and being and gave me the ability to share that love with so many countless others. You see, when you do anything with love, it makes you reach heights like never before. That's how motherhood made me who I am today.

# Ready, Set, Go—The Great Motherhood Race

*(Mum who says, "Take it one day
at a time and enjoy the Experience")*

**– Fatima Khanom –**

*(European Regional Head at a Law Firm,
IP Expert & Legal Academic)*

My partner and I have never allowed ourselves to be straight-jacketed into following society's timeline. We met fairly young, married soon thereafter, and continued our academics before embarking upon our careers. We decided, rather early on, that parenthood would be a topic that would be revisited when I entered my thirties as I discerned that my twenties was the period that I needed to grow professionally as well as personally. Furthermore, my partner is Indian, and we live mostly in India, so the cultural transition for me was admittedly an added component to this deliberation.

Fortunately, we are bestowed with considerate family, on both sides, who have never felt an imperative desire to impress upon us their own views apropos our plans for parenthood. Funnily enough, that came from well-meaning outsiders who seemed unable to fathom the idea of not assuming this conventional next step. I resigned myself to the idea that, perhaps, this limitation was rooted in their own world views and, therefore, we did not allow it to deter us from our own traction.

Parenthood appears to mandate careful contemplation, much like a trapeze artist balancing on a tightrope. Children necessitate considerable qualitative as well as quantitative resources, and there may be an overwhelming desire thrust upon parents to strive for perfection, much to their own detriment. I have been fortunate to witness up close friends and family that have or currently are striking a balance of raising well-rounded, happy children without losing their own identities. What is notable is that there is no set formula that can be applied as no set of parent(s) or offspring(s) or even circumstances are the same. This wealth of preceding experiences can act, at most, as knowledge markers at each juncture throughout a child's development. Further, with time, scientific understanding evolves in areas including child safety and behavioural methods, which demands that parents, in turn, adapt and incorporate them.

I was well entrenched in my mid-thirties when we welcomed our child during the height of the SARS-CoV-2 pandemic. It has been a double-edged sword; the worries are heightened at each wave, yet work from home has allowed invaluable quality time together that would not have happened otherwise. I am privileged to have had an extended support system comprising of medical health care and early education professionals who are a quick phone call or message away to provide any reassurances. Technology, during this pandemic, has certainly been a shot in the arm, reducing physical distance and facilitating access to an assortment of services from the comfort and safety of our homes.

At the outset, we had decided on the style of parenting we hoped to adopt, and while we are flexible about adapting, depending upon the circumstances, we plan to be as hands-on as possible. We both believe in equal parenting with equitable distribution of responsibilities as we value the importance of both parents' roles in a child's cognitive development and we would, together, need to find that balance, particularly now that we are both back at work.

Furthermore, it is vital to maintain some form of personal care to re-centre oneself, and I have been heedful of my need for respite by taking short windows of time out to do yoga, sketching or reading. It is easy to let this aspect of downtime fall by the wayside. As parents, we lead by example and should inculcate in our children the concept of the multifaceted nature of their parents' identity outside the sphere of parenthood and careers.

I recognise the propitious course that my life has taken and deem it critical not to internalise expectations and conform to parenthood until and unless one is ready. It is, after all, not a race. Moreover, I understand that there is no "one-size fits all" blueprint for raising a child or how to function as the 'perfect' parent. It will simply be an imperfect balance that we will have to muddle through. For now, I shall be savouring motherhood and treasuring these moments that seem to fly by all too swiftly.

## Prioritise Your Partner

Bringing children into the family dynamic does change it, but always for the better. I believe children strengthen the bond between partners and enrich the relationship's aura by adding a new dimension to it. However, having one-on-one time with your spouse/ partner is still incredibly important. My husband and I make it a point to do regular couple activities together, like, movie nights, dinners, etc. and, just in general, spend time together as a couple.

# I Want To Be Like My Mum

*(I am nothing like my mother)*

**– Coco Wong –**

*(Award Winning leader in Children's Entrepreneurship)*

My mother is pretty, stylish, smart, outgoing, sociable, friendly, loveable, speaks her mind, an action taker, able to influence people, loves being surrounded by people, and the list goes on. A true extrovert.

I, on the other hand, am shy, scruffy (most of the time), scare people when they first meet me (because of my straight, sometimes mistaken for grumpy, face), keep thoughts to myself, prefer sitting at home, don't really speak in gatherings and generally consider myself unfriendly. I am an introvert.

Then, there is my sister, she has the exact traits of my mum (except for the quick temper, which I got!).

As a young girl, hardly anyone notices me. Every time we met up with Aunties* and Uncles* (not necessarily relatives, it is just how we showed respect and called friends of my parents or anyone who we feel are old enough to be in their generation), they would always say to my sister "such a pretty little thing" and then turn to look at me, smile and turn back to my sister.

I did not understand why my mum and my sister were able to talk about anything under the sun whilst I struggled to have any conversation with anyone. No one wanted to talk to me much, and I would end up sitting at the dinner table all night without saying one word.

I wanted to be noticed, and I wanted to be like my mum.

One hot Summer's day, my mum took me and some friends to Ocean Park (a famous theme park in Hong Kong) and whilst we went onto a ride that just spins and spins up in the air, my mum waited down below for us. After a few spins, we started to feel a little dizzy and were wondering when the ride would stop.

Lo and behold, as I looked down at the control booth, I saw my mother sitting happily inside, chatting to the controller, and I thought, "oh no, the man has forgotten to stop the ride because he is chatting to Mum!!" (Those were the days when rides were manually controlled). She had managed to persuade the man to let her into his booth where there was air-conditioning !! That's how good my mum is at persuading people to do things.

I wanted the ability to persuade & influence people, and I wanted to be like my mum.

My mum has a super quick temper; she would go around scolding people left, right and centre. Not quite loveable, you might think, but on the contrary, this ability to speak her mind and scold and then still be loveable is quite a unique skill she has. For some reason, no matter how much she scolded people (she always says that she is not 'scolding', but it's just her way of speaking), she is able to get them to still love her and do things for her. She is never scared of losing people by speaking her mind. She is always her authentic self with nothing to hide.

I have always been scared to tell people how I felt, fear of being laughed at or criticised, fear of looking stupid, fear of being wrong, fears that paralysed me and stopped me from being my true self. I have always been secretly envious of my sister, who could speak her mind and ask for anything and get what she wanted, whilst I have been too shy even to ask, so I never got what I really wanted.

I wanted so many times to be authentic and speak my mind and ask for what I wanted, and I wanted to be like my mum.

And because of her quick temper, she is also super impatient. So when she wants you to do something, you had better get things done quickly! Sometimes, my dad might say that my mum didn't think before she took action (my dad's mantra is 'think before you do'), but to my mum, it is 'get it done NOW'. Yes, sometimes there are failures, but her mantra is 'that the word 'no' does not exist in her dictionary' so when she wants something, she finds a way to get it.

I have always been a thinker (I guess many introverts are) and would go through scenario after scenario before I would take action. Sometimes, this led to losing out or not doing anything at all.

I wanted to be able to take action quickly and find ways to do things even if it seemed impossible, and I wanted to be like my mum.

So, when I became a mum, I didn't want my children to be like me. I wanted them to be like my mum. I started to recall all those memories from my growing up and pushed myself to do what my mum would do.

And the funny thing is, as a mum with a thousand things that we need to navigate each day, being authentic and fearless became a necessity. It was just faster to be that. And by being authentic and fearless, it was easier to talk to people, they started noticing me and asking for my opinions and thoughts.

Being authentic also means that we do not need to put up a supermum 'front'. Being honest with our weaknesses will let others know we need help.

Wouldn't you agree that when we let people know we need help, they are more likely to come and help?

Also, when there is no time to fear, our animal instincts become very sharp, and with that, we are able to achieve much more in s shorter period of time. Even when we make a mistake, it is a 'faster' mistake because, in the end, even if we think about it, we might still make the same decision which results in the same mistake, so failing faster and earlier is also a better way to get good outcomes.

As a result, I can see that my daughters are growing these skills in their own ways. Children are watching us all the time. We need to be what we want them to be.

I wanted them to be like my mum, and I realised that I am My Mum now (ok, I am still scruffy, that bit didn't change – yet). What would you like your children to be like?

www.ingramcontent.com/pod-product-compliance
Lightning Source LLC
LaVergne TN
LVHW051223200726
843510LV00011B/1467